SPELLING FOR PARENTS

SPELLING FOR PARENTS

How To Help Your Child

Jo Phenix and Doreen Scott-Dunne

Piccadilly Press • London

We dedicate this book to our parents, Maisie and Joe Phenix, and Molly and David Anderson.
Our parents were our best teachers. They gave us an appreciation for language and learning that has lasted far beyond our school years. They involved us, inspired us, and encouraged us; supported us in our failures, and remained ever confident that we would realize our full potential. Across the years and across the ocean, they still rejoice in our achievements.
Thank you, Mums and Dads.

Jo Phenix is from England but now lives in Canada. She has taught children of all ages in England and Canada. She has also taught special courses in language to teachers. She now works as a writer, consultant and speaker.

Doreen Scott-Dunne is from Scotland but *now* also lives in Canada. She is a reading specialist and former consultant in language arts and drama. She has done graduate work in spelling at the Ontario Institute for Studies in Education.

Printed and bound in Great Britain by
Biddles Ltd, Guildford and King's Lynn

Contents

Notes

Foreword

When we both started teaching, the Friday spelling test was an almost universal event in our primary schools, as much a part of the classroom ritual as the national anthem. On each day of the week, prescribed exercises in spelling took place in preparation for this test. On Monday, the previous week's words could be abandoned as children prepared for the next list of random words. Three times a year, parents read in their children's report cards that "spelling is improving, but there is no carry-over in the writing." In time we realized that this memorization game was not teaching children much about spelling.

At the same time, we began using a new and more liberal approach to writing in our schools. Instead of prescribing topics and focusing almost exclusively on the accuracy of spelling, grammar, and punctuation, we shifted our focus to composition and creativity. After an initial period of wariness, children wrote as never before. The quantity increased, the topics proliferated, and language and vocabulary knew no bounds.

A similar revolution was taking place in our reading periods, as we moved from controlled vocabulary and stilted texts to real children's literature, from total teacher control to independent reading and shared responsibility. Reflection and personal response took the place of written comprehension questions.

Those of us who have been involved in this return to natural language learning and real-life language experiences are in no doubt that children have become better readers and writers and more proficient users of language as a result. Research has taught us a lot about how children learn, about how language is learned, about what kinds of experiences are necessary for successful learning. The rigid, old methods had to give way to new approaches which more closely match real-life experience.

What we have done in our classrooms is to put into practice what parents have always known about language and learning. When our children first start to talk, we don't sit them down and teach them rules. Nor do we correct them every time they make a mistake, or feel there is a problem if they are not accurate in every detail. We involve them in what we are doing; we talk to them in a natural way; we listen to what they have to say; and we respond to what they are trying to tell us, even if we can only pick up a few words here and there. At the same time our children are listening to the language around them, learning more about words and how they are used, and putting what they hear into practice. Children learn to speak because parents instinctively know that language is learned by using it to do everyday things, and that it is learned gradually, step by step, over a long period of time. This is what we in teaching call developmental learning, the natural process of gradually getting closer to standard English.

The skills we want our children to learn have not

changed. We want them to be good users of language in all its forms, written and oral, receptive and expressive. As a result of our new understandings about language learning, we have widened our goals. We put a premium on content in writing, and teach children to work as real writers do, through a process of drafts and revisions. We value real substance over superficial accuracy. We try to respond to their efforts in a supportive way, and encourage experimentation and risk-taking.

None of this means we need to exclude a focus on spelling. Spelling is a part of the writing process, a part of life. Once children feel free to write, have something to say, and language to express their ideas, then we must teach them how to present their writing in standard forms of spelling. Quantity writing is only part of the learning process; helping children learn as much as possible through this writing must be our goal.

It seems to be a common misconception that schools and teachers no longer value or teach correct spelling. This is not true. Certainly other aspects of writing now receive more emphasis than before; composition is given its due priority as the heart and soul of the writing process. Spelling, however, has a vital role to play. There needs to be a balance in teaching to help children understand the place of spelling, and have enough confidence as spellers so that they are not inhibited as writers.

1. An Introduction to Spelling

The Mythology of Spelling

There are a number of myths supporting the belief that spelling cannot be successfully taught or learned. These myths need to be dispelled.

Myth 1
Some people can spell and some people can't, and that's the way it is.

There is no parallel myth that there are people who can read and people who can't, and there is not much we can do about it. It is certainly true that some people have more trouble with spelling than others. We don't give up on people who cannot read, so why should we give up on those who cannot spell?

Myth 2
There is no logic to English spelling, so why even try?

This myth is reinforced when people point out different

ways of spelling the same sound, and spellings that are irregular. Some older children who are chronically poor spellers give up completely, and, in extreme cases, revert to writing strings of random letters; they believe they have no chance of ever spelling correctly, no matter what they try. *What children need to learn is that there are only a limited number of alternatives for spelling a word, not an infinite number of possibilities.* It is important that all children come to understand that the English system of spelling is basically logical, having rational and historical explanations for its differing patterns. This understanding can help dispel a third myth:

Myth 3
Learning to spell is a rote-memory process.

This myth has been perpetuated by many spelling texts and much spelling instruction. Such texts have often been based on the 3000 most common words, which children were asked to memorize through weekly lists. Often, the words on the lists had no spelling link with one another; the lessons provided activities designed to help memorization. Those children who could memorize words for a test often misspelled these same words in their writing.

Contemporary researchers have redefined spelling, not as a low-level, rote-memorization task, but instead as a high-level cognitive skill. This means that spelling and thinking go hand in hand. To be able to spell, you have to know a great deal about the English language, and be able to apply this knowledge to the construction of words.

Myth 4
If you are a poor speller, you are a poor writer.

Because society puts a high premium on standard spelling, many poor spellers have drawn the conclusion that spelling is the major skill in writing. As a consequence, they believe themselves to be poor writers. Of course, if we want to make a good impression, we want our spelling to be perfect before our writing goes on public view. This is the purpose of copy editing and proof-reading. It is important, though, not to confuse spelling and composition. Composition is the creation of writing, involving having something to say, someone to say it to, and the language with which to say it. This must be done first, before there is any need for spelling.

Being a poor speller does not detract from the quality of a person's ideas or the flow of language. The only real spelling requirement for early drafts is that the writer can read back what has been written. The greatest tragedy of spelling occurs when it presents a barrier to writing. While we recognize the importance of spelling, we need to put it in perspective and understand where it fits in the writing process.

Myth 5
There are right and wrong ways to spell.

Most of us have at some time been surprised, not to mention horrified, to discover that there are alternate ways to spell words – that there isn't always one right way. People are often bothered by regional and national differences in spelling, believing that there is "our way and the wrong way."

The truth is that spelling is something we made up when we started to keep records. The concept of standard spelling is a relatively new one. Standard spelling is a consensus, not a rule, and is constantly evolving. At any one time, many words are in a process of change, some people using the old way, some adopting the new. Dictionaries recognize this and list the alternatives that are in use. We should not be smug about right and wrong in spelling.

Myth 6
It is not necessary to teach spelling.

The failure of some past methods of spelling instruction has led some teachers to believe that spelling instruction is a waste of time. Certainly, children should not be spending time on repetitive rote-memory tasks in preparation for a weekly test, but there are many spelling concepts which can be learned, and which can form the basis of creative instruction. What we need is a new understanding of what the skills of spelling are. If we couple this understanding with our knowledge of how language is learned and practised, then we can help children to be better spellers.

The Chauvinism of Spelling

Both of us grew up in Britain where the Oxford English

Dictionary is the guardian of "truth" about spelling. In Britain, American spelling is considered a bastardization of the "right" way. In the United States, spelling has certainly undergone more changes, some evolutionary, others deliberate and revolutionary. Now we live in Canada, a country of a certain spelling ambivalence. Some words are spelled the English way, some the American way. As if this were not confusing enough, different parts of the country favour or favor different spellings. Even publishers of books and newspapers within the same city may use different spelling guides. If you use an English or an American dictionary you know what you are getting, however, with a Canadian dictionary you take your chances. How is it possible to know what is right? Which version of spelling should we be teaching?

Spelling, like all forms of language, is relative to the user and to the situation. Most of us read books published in all parts of the English-speaking world. When children read widely, they will notice differences in spellings. They should be encouraged to see this as an example of the flexibility and diversity of language customs, rather than as a problem. Even young children readily learn that they must use different language in different situations: their playground language is not the same as their classroom language, and they know which words they must not say when an adult is listening. Teenagers develop entirely new dialects and vocabularies that change so rapidly many adults feel they cannot communicate with them.

Regional and national dialects used to be considered a problem, something to be eradicated so that everyone would use the same standard speech. In 19th-century England, and well into the 20th century, using the standard dialect was one way of moving up in society, showing that you belonged to the educated classes. Many classrooms today bring together children and adults with vastly different dialects of English, and our attitudes have changed. Now we do our best to have children value and maintain their native speech while being aware of, and able to operate in, standard English. Rather than changing their dialect, we add another to it.

There is always the question of what is standard English. It is certainly not the same in Cheltenham, Chiliwak, and Chatanooga. Isn't it always the other person who has the dialect? One definition is that standard English is the dialect used by the dominant professional class of the region in which you happen to live. It is often exemplified by news readers on your local television station. Standard English is also relative.

We need to teach children that language and spelling vary according to region and nationality. We can then give them options to use when they are making spelling decisions. There are two choices:

1. *Pick a dictionary and stick with it.*
If you live in Chatanooga and you decide the Oxford English Dictionary is for you, people can say you are quaint and old-fashioned, but they cannot say you are wrong. The sensible choice, however, is to discover the consensus according to where you live and go with the majority.

2.*Vary your spelling according to your audience.*
This is difficult because most of us are very protective of our own spelling customs and believe that our way is the

right way. The sophisticated speller, however, knows that spelling is for the reader, not the writer. You might use English or American spelling according to what you would expect your reader to use. If your reader is Canadian, good luck.

The History of Spelling

You have probably heard that Shakespeare spelt his name at least seven different ways. Perhaps you feel you too would like to have the option of spelling words any way you like. You might still be able to do that today, except for the influence of three men: William Caxton, Samuel Johnston, and Noah Webster. They began the process of formalizing and standardizing written English, first through the invention of the printing press, and later through the creation of dictionaries.

The Printing Press

Until the late Middle Ages, books were rare and had to be copied by hand. The only book most people saw was the Bible, chained in the church. Few people ever saw the printed word – there were no spelling problems. Then, in 1476, the printing press was invented. For the first time in history, people had access to standardized spelling, that is, the spelling chosen by William Caxton, the first printer of the English language. Because Caxton worked in London, he made an arbitrary decision to print the variety of English spoken in London at that time.

There are many spellings Caxton used that we would not employ today, for example:

langage for language   *frenshe* for French
certaynly for certainly   *sayd* for said
englysshe for English   *sayled* for sailed

Because of the limitations of the printing press, Caxton made some practical changes, for example, he changed the *u* to *o* in words like *done, come, wonder,* and *love* because his press would not print a good, clean *u*.

Although the printing press brought about some standardization of spelling, the idea of Standard English was still very much in its infancy. Other printers established businesses and used different varieties of spoken and written English. Books published in the 16th century reflect the language of their publishers and the regions in which they lived and worked. However, by the time the 1611 version of the Bible was published, the words were much closer to today's spelling, although you can still see the influence of Chaucer's time in words such as these:

shepheard for shepherd
greene for green
walke for walk
oyle for oil
cuppe for cup
shadowe for shadow

This may be because Caxton had been the first to print Chaucer's works.

The Dictionary

In 1604, a man called Robert Cawdray produced a dictionary of 120 pages called, "A Table Alphabeticall," which he wrote for "Ladies ... or any other unskilfull persons"!

Samuel Johnson published his dictionary in 1755. It was produced in nine years by Johnson and six assistants working like Bob Cratchet in a garret. In the dictionary, he defined 40,000 words, along with analogies and quotations. Although it was noted for its scholarship and the detail and accuracy of the definitions, this dictionary is probably just as memorable for the sparkle of Johnson's wit:

> *Pension* An allowance made to anyone without an equivalent. In England it is generally understood to mean pay given to a state hireling for treason to his country.

> *Oats* A grain, which in England is generally given to horses, but in Scotland supports the people.[1]

It was Johnson's opinion that English spelling tended to favour meaning over sound, and in most cases he made an attempt to spell homophones (bare, bear) differently. However, he did list *flower* with two meanings – "blossom" and "meal."

One of the reasons Dr Johnson wrote a dictionary was

---

[1] To which Boswell replied: "Which is why England is famous for its horses, and Scotland for its men."

his wish that future generations would be able to read Shakespeare's writings, that they would not be lost because of a spelling system which did not reflect changes in pronunciation. His wish came true.

For the new middle class which arose during the industrial revolution, the dictionary was a way to improve one's station in life. Dialect became not only an indication of where one lived, but a mark of social class. For a social climber of Victorian England, speaking and writing "the Queen's English" conferred respectability and a sense of belonging. In the preface to *Pygmalion*, George Bernard Shaw remarked that "it is impossible for an Englishman to open his mouth without making some other Englishman despise him."

On the other side of the Atlantic, in 1828, Noah Webster compiled the first dictionary of American English, one-third larger than Dr Johnson's, which set the spelling standard for English-speaking Americans. He also made some arbitrary decisions to change some of the spellings. Examples of his spelling reforms included the following:

color for colour	*defense* for defence
wagon for waggon	*music* for musick
robin for robbin	*tire* for tyre

Although Webster was trying to simplify spelling, he was responsible for creating some new problems. In English spelling, there is a standard pattern that in a word of more than one syllable, when a consonant follows a short vowel, the consonant is doubled, as in *little, Mummy, Daddy, dinner, happy, rabbit, yellow, sunny, letter*, and so on. In his effort to simplify spelling, Webster created two new exceptions: *wagon* and *robin*. He went on to wage a one-man crusade to change spelling. Webster would visit printers with his new spellings written on cards, asking them to please, in future, spell the words his way.

Today, spelling is considered correct or incorrect based on arbitrary and sometimes illogical decisions made by one printer and two writers of dictionaries.

How Language Changes

Although dictionaries standardized spelling, the English language is far from static. Johnson included 40,000 words in his dictionary; Shakespeare used 30,000 words in his writing. In comparison, an educated person today would be unlikely to use a vocabulary of more than 15,000 words. It seems apt that Shakespeare added the word *multitudinous* to our vocabulary.[1] Today, when a new word is created, there is an outcry in the press about the corruption of the language.

Lewis Carroll began the creation of portmanteau words – words which have two meanings packed into one, such as *chortle*, a combination of chuckle and snort. Portmanteau words are extremely popular today:

> *bit* (binary + digit)
> *brunch* (breakfast + lunch)
> *motel* (motor + hotel)
> *transistor* (transfer + resistor)

---

[1] He also added *dislocate, obscene, critical, emphasis, initiate, modest, horrid, vast, submerged, assassination,* and many more.

As well as blending words together to create new words, we sometimes clip words, dropping the longer form and using the shorter form. Examples include:

wig from periwig
cello from violoncello
taxi from taxicab

We also create new words by changing nouns into verbs:

breakfast to breakfasted
golf to golfed
bus to bussed[1]

or verbs into nouns:

to break down into *breakdown*
to fall out into *fall-out*
to hold up into *hold-up*

As well as changing the shape and function of words over the years, we have in some cases changed their meaning. Sometimes we narrow the meaning of a word. Until the 16th century, the word *deer* meant any kind of animal, and was not limited to a particular type of hoofed animal. This gives new significance to the death penalty imposed on peasants for killing the King's deer – it meant they could die for any kind of poaching. Sometimes we widen the meaning. *Board* was once limited to meaning "a

---

[1] And the writing teacher's favourite: *conferenced.* We thought the verb was "to confer."

piece of timber," lacking the range of meanings it has today:

> meals served in exchange for payment or services
> the distance sailed by a ship on one tack
> the wall surrounding the ice in hockey
> the backboard behind the basket in basketball

not to mention *boarder, surfboard, baseboard, boardwalk,* and the *Board of Education.*

Another way we change words is by combining two separate words into one – compounding words:

searchlight	snowman
overkill	splashdown
highway	blackbird
breakfast	hotplate

Sometimes words change in meaning because of incorrect usage. The word *apron* used to be spelled *napron* People constantly heard *a napron* and thought it was *an apron,* and so the spelling changed.

North Americans have recently changed the meaning of *momentarily.* It is formed from the adjective, *momentary,* meaning fleeting or brief. The 1987 Webster's dictionary defines *momentarily* as "lasting for a moment," but it is almost universally used to mean "in a moment." This probably came about because of a desire to sound more literate by using a long word instead of a short one. We still worry when we are told the aeroplane will be landing momentarily.

It will be interesting to note how long it takes for this

change in meaning to be reflected in the dictionary. A dictionary, after all, does not *pre*scribe as much as *de*scribe language as it is used.

This explains why for many words there are two or more acceptable spellings. If enough people use a word incorrectly, either in its spelling or in its meaning, for a long enough period, the incorrect spelling eventually becomes legitimate. You may like to become a kind of spelling anthropologist, and study changes in spelling. We have noticed, for example, that the *gue* ending is in the process of disappearing. We often see the words *catalog*, *monolog*, *dialog*, and *epilog*, and our Webster's gives these as alternate spellings. It does not, however, give any alternate spelling for *synagogue*. How long will it be before *gue* becomes the alternate? How long before *ue* disappears?

The English language is constantly growing, changing, and becoming more complex. Yet for over 150 years, the spelling of most words has remained the same. The pronunciation of many words has strayed further and further from their original link to sound – the *w* in *two* and the *b* in *tomb* used to be pronounced, but are now silent.[1] Consequently, the more we know about the origins and evolution of our language, the more chance we have of figuring out how our spelling system works, and how we can master it.

---

[1] The *w* in *two* is still pronounced in Scotland, as is the *h* in *where*.

Attempts to Simplify Spelling

Attempts to simplify spelling go back as far as the Middle Ages. In the 15th century, a monk named Ormin tried to make spelling more closely reflect pronunciation. In the 16th century, a Cambridge professor, Sir John Cheke, tried to get rid of silent letters. In the 17th century, another Cambridge master and later bishop, proposed an international phonetic alphabet. In the 18th century, Benjamin Franklin published a paper called, "A Scheme For a New Alphabet and a Reformed Mode of Spelling." At least part of his purpose was to reinforce the concept of an independent America through independence in language. His ideas were not widely accepted, but he was responsible for these spellings: *honor, theater, plow,* and *curb.* Franklin devised another phonetic alphabet, but he did not publish it, claiming he was too old for a crusade. He was a realist; none of the earlier attempts to simplify spelling had had any measure of success. In the 19th century, Charles Darwin, who we thought understood the laws of natural selection, became associated, along with Alfred, Lord Tennyson, with the British Spelling Reform Association.

In 20th-century England, the British Simplified Spelling Society tried, without success, to get government support for spelling reforms. George Bernard Shaw advocated simplified spelling, leaving part of his fortune for this purpose. In America, Andrew Carnegie financed the Simplified Spelling Board, which proposed 300 new spellings. Theodore Roosevelt endorsed some of these, and ordered their use in the Government Printing Office. When Roosevelt was defeated by Taft, *The New York Sun* announced the event with a one-word headline: *THRU*.

Noah Webster was at first conservative about spelling, opposing any changes. Later, he did try some simplification, publishing words like *thum, iland, hed, giv, bilt, iz, mashine, yeer,* and *wimmen* These were retracted in later versions. He was successful in introducing the following: *physic(k), center, theater, honor, favor, traveled, check, mask,* and *defense.*

Despite many attempts, often by well-known and influential people, simplified spelling has never been widely accepted. One problem is that once the spelling of a word has changed, it loses its etymology, and hence, its reason for existence. Spelling has as much to do with meaning as with sound. Phonetic spelling would destroy meaning links between words, such as *mnemonic* and *amnesia, sign* and *signature.* Dialect is another complication.

Perhaps the most serious problem is that people have never been able to agree on which changes are desirable – or even whether change is necessary. After all, who decides? Most prefer that evolution make the decisions for us. There may also be an element of guilt, a feeling that we *ought* to be able to spell, and that making it easier is somehow giving in.

Or do we just like our spelling system the way it is?

The Logic of Spelling

We tend to think of English as a non-phonetic language, composed of totally illogical spellings and pronunciations. Because there are so many different ways to represent the sounds of the language, we may regard spelling as difficult and unpredictable.

In fact, our spelling system is not totally random. We do not have to rely only on memory. A good speller is not a person who has successfully memorized the most words, but rather someone who knows ways to figure out the logic of words and can construct them as needed. Spelling is problem solving with letters, sounds, patterns, and meanings.

In a way, spelling is rather like trying to find your way around a strange city with the help of a road map. If you know how maps work, and can follow a few basic principles, you can not only find your way, but feel in control of the situation. Even if you get lost once in a while, you can get back on track.

There are three major principles you have to understand in order to use the road map of spelling:

the pattern by sound or alphabetic principle;
the pattern by function principle;
the pattern by meaning principle.

Pattern By Sound

One of the problems with spelling is that there are only 26 letters in the alphabet, but more than 40 sounds in spoken English. If we were inventing a language from scratch, we would probably have a symbol for every sound. (Of course, to do this we would have to eliminate dialect: in the south of England, *bath* and *hearth* rhyme; in the north they do not.) Another problem is that we often spell the same sound in different ways, such as the *f* sound in *far*, *phone*, and *laugh*, and the *u* sound in *nut*, *tough*, *done*, and *blood*.

Nevertheless, many of the sounds in words do correspond to letters or groups of letters. The sound-symbol relationships are predictable for the most part, and follow known patterns. Children begin to spell by using their knowledge of the names of letters, and what they hear when they make sounds in the mouth:

are is written as *r*; *you* as *u*;

gate is written as *gat*, because they hear *a* in the middle;

pin is written as *pen* because a short *i* sounds most like the letter *e*;

drum is written as *jrum*, because they hear *j* at the beginning;

laugh is written *laf* , because they hear only one sound at the end of the word.

When young children write, they concentrate on representing the sounds themselves, thus adhering to the alphabetic principle. As they become more knowledgeable about words, they are reassured to discover that there are patterns in spelling.

• Most consonant sounds are represented by the letter you expect:

If it sounds like *t*, it probably is *t*.

• In many words the sound-symbol relationship is highly predictable:

dad, remember, prehistoric

• There are many clusters of words which share the same sound-symbol pattern:

gate, state, relate, berate, stagnate, delegate
seat, cheat, neat, treat, beater, defeat, creature

• There are patterns related to the sequence of letters in a word:

We always use *qu* for a *kw* sound at the beginning of words.

• Some sounds are represented by two letters:

shape, shop, smash
chin, check, church

This alphabetic principle allows us to make a reasonable attempt at spelling most words. All we need to know is which combination of letters are probable, which are possible, which are improbable, and which are impossible.[1]

Pattern By Function

Many patterns relate to how a word is used – the function it serves in a sentence. This is how it works:

---

[1] For more about probables, possibles, improbables, and impossibles, see p. 24

If you were to rely on sound only, you would spell the past tense of *walked*, *waited*, and *warned* as *walkt*, *waitid*, and *warnd*.

We know that this is not right because *ed* is a past-tense marker: the sound may change, but the spelling does not.[1]

Our spelling system signals the past tense graphically. This pattern is not only logical, it is helpful in reading. It can also be a helpful pattern in spelling. If you can apply it correctly to one word, then you can apply it to them all.

Other examples of pattern by function are plurals, possessives, and contractions. Once you know the pattern, you can apply it in new situations.

Some spelling patterns are structural markers; the presence of one or more letters affects the pronunciation of others, for example, *hop* and *hope*, *hoping* and *hopping*, and *courageous* (soft *g*).

We know that young children are learning function patterns in speech when they say words like *wented* and *goed*. This tells us that they have made a generalization about the structure of past-tense verbs, and can apply this knowledge in new situations. They will make similar generalizations about usage patterns when they are learning to spell.

Pattern By Meaning

Often the meaning of a word helps us with the spelling. Meaning is linked to derivation, the use of affixes to build words from a root or base, often with a change in the part of speech:

---

[1] There are only a few exceptions to the *ed* rule, for example: *spelt*, *blest*, *dwelt*, *burnt*.

| predict | prediction | contradiction | interdiction |
| like | likely | unlikely | likelihood |

Even when pronunciation changes, the spelling does not:

please	pleasant
revise	revision
medicine	medical
nation	national

Even when emphasis changes, the spelling does not:

derive	derivation

Knowing that words are derived from the same base helps us put in letters we would otherwise omit:

autumn	autumnal
condemn	condemnation
solemn	solemnity
mnemonic	amnesia
sign	signal
design	designate
muscle	muscular

Knowing how to add a prefix can help us avoid some of the most misspelled words:

mis spell
de siccate

As we build a knowledge of common prefixes, suffixes,

and root words, we add to the information we can call on to help us spell.

Following the Road Map

Using these three kinds of information in combination helps us to create words we need to spell. Learning to spell is not just a matter of memorizing words. None of us learned all the words we can spell by memorization. We must keep the number of words we have to memorize as low as possible.

Spelling is a skill of constructing words.

Once we know the three main roads of spelling, more experience with language will help us recognize the dead-end streets and the exceptions to predictable patterns. Misreading the map is not a major problem because we can monitor our progress, ask directions, retrace our steps, self-correct, and start again.

If children understand how the spelling system works, they feel they have some control over it. A feeling of control can enable one to manipulate language with a reasonable chance of using it accurately. Spelling will no longer be a maze children wander blindly through, but a series of problems they can use good strategies to solve.

2. How Spelling Is Learned

What Good Spellers Don't Know They Know

You may have seen the following phonic joke written by George Bernard Shaw.

What is this word?
ghoti
Here are the phonic rules for you to sound it out:
gh as in *rough*
o as in *women*
ti as in *nation*

Isn't it strange how difficult sounding out is when you don't know the word?

The really interesting point, though, is the word *ghoti*. We all know that this could not possibly be an English word because of its appearance. The estimated number of words in the English language is about two million, depending on how many scientific words and derivations you decide to include. In our lives, we will meet only a fraction of these words. A quick browse through a medium-sized dictionary reveals hundreds of words we have never seen. How do we know, then, that *ghoti* could not be an English word?

Well, we know that *gh* does not make the sound of *f* at the beginnings of words. It sometimes does in the middle or at the end, but *never* at the beginning. None of us learned this in school. Even the most dedicated and thorough of phonics teachers did not think of this rule, yet we all know it. This rule is one of the hundreds of generalizations we have made about language through our reading and writing. Most of the time we are not aware of it, but it is this kind of intrinsic knowledge about how words are supposed to look – what is possible and what is impossible – that enables us to spell.

A good speller is a person who has a sense of what is probable, what is possible, what is improbable, and what is impossible in English spelling. This is how we make predictions about how words are likely to be spelled.[1] There are so many generalizations that we could not attempt to teach them all, even if we could work out what they are. What we can do is help children increase their awareness and make their own generalizations by doing the following activities.

• Have them read, read, read. Spelling patterns are largely visual, and we want children to see the patterns of

---

[1] We first heard this concept of a sliding scale from probability to impossibility when talking in the early 1980s with a former colleague, Chris Worsnop. He says he got it from his reading of Aristotle's *Poetics*. Worsnop believed then, and still does, that the errors people make in spelling can be assessed according to this scale, and would like to use the concept in a research project.

words over and over again.

• Help them to express themselves through oral language. Enunciation and pronunciation are also important to spelling. An awareness of correct pronunciation can prevent errors in words like *February* and *government*.

• Encourage children to write for many purposes: shopping lists, letters, phone messages, postcards. Every time they write, they will practise word construction.

• Take every opportunity to help children look for patterns and similarities in words. Though we cannot teach all the patterns, we can teach the *concept* that patterns are there to be discovered.

• Engage children's interest in words and language. The more they question and investigate, the more they will learn about the possibles, the probables, the improbables, and the impossibles of spelling.

The word in the puzzle is *fish*.

How We Have Taught Spelling in the Past

The Practical Speller, published by Gage and Company in 1881, bemoans in its preface the demise of the old-fashioned Spelling Book, stating that, "They took our bread and have given in return but a stone. The bread even though a little stale was much more wholesome than the stone." It seems spelling was in poor shape then: " ... pupils are turned loose on society to shock it by their bad spelling, and disgrace the schools which they attended, and in which they should have been taught." In a Civil Service Exam of the time in England, "no less than 1861 out of 1972 failures were caused by spelling."

The Practical Speller's answer to this is a book of themed word lists and passages for dictation. There is no attempt to group together words with common spelling patterns. There are no lesson plans or strategies, just the lists. The teaching emphasis is on articulation and seeing with precision: the implication is clear that correct teaching is the answer to all problems. Words and dictations are to be written on the slates to imprint the look of the word on the children's minds. Some of the suggested strategies seem more modern. As examples, there is space for the children to make their own word lists, and the importance of reading is emphasized, along with the statement, "It is desirable that spelling should be taught to a considerable extent by means of composition, in order to give the pupils practice in spelling the words in their own vocabularies."

This memorization of word lists has been the common pattern for most spelling instruction in the past. Many of us remember the weekly or weakly spelling bees that were held, in which we were forced to display our knowledge, or lack thereof, before our classmates. We were placed in a situation of high anxiety and embarrassment that made the task difficult, even for good spellers. It is unlikely that this taught us much about spelling: we learned nothing new as we paraded only existent knowledge. Moreover, as spelling is primarily a visual skill, and we never got to see the words, important information about spelling patterns had no chance to become imprinted on our minds.

As we grew older, learning to spell was a matter of correcting all the errors we made in our writing.

Occasionally, we had to write the words three times at the bottom, as a way of aiding our memories. The teacher did all the proof-reading, marking errors with a "sp" in the margin, and writing comments about "careless mistakes." Of course, this was always single-draft writing, in which we were supposed to make everything come out perfect the first time.

Newer methods of instruction recognize the visual nature of spelling by teaching study steps such as the following: look at the word, picture it in your mind, look away and write the word, look back and check. If a word cannot be linked into a pattern, and rote memorization is the only strategy available, this may help in the short term. However, this kind of rote-memory work is only useful if the word is then used frequently enough for it to pass into long-term memory. Frequent usage is more likely to bring about learning than the study steps. One dangerous side-effect of this study-step method is that it focuses attention on learning one word at a time, rather than on making spelling links. If the study-step method is used frequently, it may teach children that memorization is the only way to learn to spell.

We have sometimes tried to make sense of spelling by grouping together words that are constructed in similar ways, to make "word families." A word family might be composed of rhyming words, words with the same prefix or suffix, past-tense verbs sharing the same ending, words from the same Latin or Greek root, or words which use the same group of letters, like *tch*. This makes good spelling sense, because if you know one word in the "family," you have a good chance of being able to spell the others as well. However, lists in spelling texts are commonly based not on word families, but on lists of high-frequency words. In the list, linked words are often buried among unrelated words.

Sometimes word lists seem to be designed to confuse the learner. In a recently published speller, one lesson objective is to teach that the sound *e* can be spelled *ee*, *ea*, and *ie*. If this isn't confusing enough, the word list also includes the following: *rest*, *friend*, *they*, and *yard*.

Because we recognize the importance of writing in creating the purpose for spelling, and the place of spelling as part of the writing process, many teachers get children to create personal spelling lists with words taken from their writing. Children need to spell the words they use often in their writing; if they are not using the words, why do they need to learn them? But children will only learn to make spelling generalizations if they deal with words in "spelling contexts" – groups of words which share a spelling pattern. When words are selected from a child's writing, they must be placed in their spelling contexts so that the child can make the necessary links. Getting childen to use "study steps" on unconnected words is not likely to lead to lasting learning. It results only in another list of words to be memorized.

There is another school of thought that says plenty of reading and writing are all you need to learn how to spell. If this were true, all prolific readers and writers would be good spellers. This is not the case. It is quite common for someone to be a good reader but a poor speller and vice versa. While reading and writing provide information about words, a purpose for understanding how they work, and a medium for using them, they are not enough for many people to become good spellers. Fluent readers look at very little of the visual information on the page; this explains why many good readers and spellers cannot proof-read well. Even beginner readers use context clues which enable them to figure out words and phrases without looking at all the letters or the syllables. Often, the details of words are overlooked.

There is clearly a need for a new kind of spelling instruction, one that raises children's awareness about language and its patterns, and focuses on word construction rather than word memorization.

The Spelling/Writing Connection

As soon as children begin to write, they become aware of the need for spelling. Memorizing a map of a city you have no intention of visiting would be an impossible task, not to mention an enormous waste of time. Writing gives spelling meaning.

Writing not only provides the medium for using spelling, but also a context for learning to spell. It is not enough just to write. It is of little importance if we make spelling errors on our shopping list; the important thing is whether we can read it when we get to the supermarket. To provide motivation for correct spelling, the writing must be intended for another to read. If the spelling is poor, we will make a bad impression, and may fail to communicate our true meaning. No one wants to look silly in print. For writing to be a significant factor in learning to spell, the writer must be writing for a real audience. Without an audience, there is no need for standard spelling.

The idea of teaching spelling through the children's writing has given rise to a number of misconceptions. It is a good idea to give children words they need for writing in progress: we know that if they need the words, they are more likely to learn them. However, picking out words and using them to make a personal spelling list once again reduces spelling to a rote-memory skill. We know that rote learning is the hardest way to learn, is typically short-lived, and therefore cannot be viewed as a productive strategy. Lists of "theme words" can provide a ready reference for the spellings of words and encourage children to use them, but these lists will not often provide a spelling context to help children learn the words.

Spelling errors in writing may be treated in two ways. One is a focus on proof-reading and correcting, which involves identifying words that are misspelled and replacing them with the standard spellings. The second is a focus on spelling instruction, which involves helping the child to form links between words, make new generalizations about spellings, and connect the words in some way with existing spelling knowledge. This may mean setting the word in a sound-based or word-family context with other words that look and sound the same. It may be teaching a pattern by function, such as an *ed* ending or a contraction. It may be providing a meaning link, such as *medicine* and *medical*. For long-term spelling learning to occur, the word taken from the writing must be placed in a spelling context.

Spelling should never interfere with composition; it should not be taught while the child is writing a first draft. By drawing the child's attention to spelling at inappropriate stages of the writing, we work against what we are trying to teach about the writing process. When we respond, we comment only on the focus of the task. If this was content, then that is what we talk about. If we start commenting on spelling at this stage, even to praise, then the child will learn that spelling is an important factor in first-draft writing, and must therefore be a focus at that time. This is not productive in the process of writing successfully, nor is it productive in the teaching of spelling. There is a time in the writing process when spelling will be a major focus. At this stage, we may evaluate the child's spelling, talk about it, teach about it, and expect his or her full attention. It is important to give a child one aspect to focus on at a time.

3. What to Teach About Spelling

What Spelling Is For?

Spelling is one of the less interesting and more laborious aspects of writing. It can also be the most noticeable, one that can create a good or bad impression before a reader thinks about what the writer has to say. Therefore, whether we like it or not, spelling is important.

Children will be more apt to spend time and attention on spelling and other aspects of transcription if they see a real need for it. Here are some things children need to understand:

• People will form an opinion of you based on the attractiveness and accuracy of your writing. If your spelling is incorrect, you will make a poor impression.
• If your writing is hard to read, others will often give up and not bother to finish reading your piece.
• Punctuation makes things easier to read and understand. Sometimes it can change the meaning of a sentence.
• Poor spelling can be distracting for a reader, and can make a stronger impression than your composition.

• Any kind of "noise" in the message can hinder your meaning. Poor spelling is noise.
• Sometimes a misspelling can change your meaning.

The best way for children to learn these basic truths is to have many purposes and audiences for their writing. Spelling and neatness are more for the reader than for the writer. Without a reader, they have no purpose.

Help your child understand that correct spelling and neat, attractive presentation are courtesies to the reader. They are also ways to put on your best face, to make a good impression. It is rather like cleaning house when visitors are expected, or combing your hair before having your photograph taken. There are occasions when we all want to look our best.

When Does Spelling Count?

Children need to know when spelling matters. If your child constantly asks you how to spell words or wonders, "Does spelling count?" you know that she or he has a problem. If a writer does not know whether to focus on spelling or content, then the writing cannot be successful. We want children to put time and effort into spelling when it is called for – we do not want them wasting time on it when it is not appropriate.

> To think spelling always matters is as non-productive as thinking it never matters.

As adults, we know when correctness matters. During

33

a first draft, we usually make an attempt to spell as correctly as possible; we may stop and think about a word or make a second attempt to spell it. However, we will not usually break our train of thought to fetch the dictionary; we are likely to make a note to check on the spelling later. Few bother to recopy writing that no one is going to see. If the shopping list is messy, who cares? If the list is for someone else to see, we take time to ensure neatness and correct spelling.

Children need to understand that in a final draft, standard spelling and attractive presentation are important. Up to this stage in the writing process, paying attention to composition, language use, and organization of information are far more important, and should receive the writer's full attention. This is a simple rule that children can learn. They will only learn it, though, if their writing experiences follow the rules and customs of the outside world.

The Real-World Rules of Spelling

• Spelling is never a focus of first-draft writing.
• In personal writing that only the writer will see, spelling is the writer's choice.
• You always have a chance to check your writing before you are to be judged on spelling.
• No one knows, or cares, who helped with spelling, or how many words needed to be corrected.
• Spelling is important in writing that is to go public.

You can teach the place of spelling by practising some

of the following guidelines.

• When you are looking at a piece of writing that is a first draft, or temporary, or very personal, ignore the spelling. Just show an interest in what your child is writing about. This will illustrate what you think is important at this stage.
• Do not criticize or congratulate your child on spelling in first-draft writing. Show that up to this point it does not matter. Even praise can teach the wrong lesson.
• If your child asks how to spell a word, promise to help with spelling later when the main part of the writing is done.[1]
• Find as many opportunities as you can for your child to do writing which is to be seen by someone else. This will give a legitimate purpose for careful editing and proof-reading.
• Always expect to see correct spelling and neat handwriting in a final draft. When your child is preparing writing for a final, good copy, offer all the help you can.
• Give plenty of praise for effort and achievement when a good final draft is completed.

It is important to constantly reinforce these truths about spelling. Children need to hear the same message in all subjects, from all teachers, and from their parents. No matter what the task or the topic, spelling is done the same way and for the same reasons.

---

[1] You can be more flexible once your child knows the place of spelling, and when and where to focus on it.

The Las Vegas Rules of Spelling

English spelling is noted for exceptions to rules. Many of the rules we learned in school have so many exceptions they cannot be called rules at all. It is often these exceptions that cause spelling problems. When so-called "rules" let children down, they may once again feel they have no strategies for spelling, and subsequently, no control.

A far more reliable system is to follow the Las Vegas Rules and play the odds. To understand playing the odds, consider the spelling of the sound, *shun*.

First, we can learn that at the end of a word this sound is *never* spelled *shun*. This is useful information, especially for young children who will try to spell it this way.

We have found twelve ways of spelling this sound:

tion	sion	cean	shion	tian	sian
cian	cion	chian	chion	cheon	xion

A poor speller might expect to have a very slim chance of being right – or an eleven out of twelve chance of being wrong. Not so. Look at the odds:

In eight out of nine cases, this sound is spelled *tion*.

Here are even better odds. If you hear *a-shun*, there are at least 1200 words with *ation*, and only four exceptions!

We found very few examples for some of the possible spellings:

one word ending in *chion*

two words ending in *chian*
two common words ending in *xion* (along with three
we have never seen before, much less used)
two words ending in *shion*
two words ending in *cean*
two words ending in *cion*
three words ending in *cheon*

Very few of these are common words. They can almost
be ignored.

A Las Vegas Rule for spelling the sound of shun
therefore would be:

If in doubt, choose tion.

If you do this, you will be right 88 per cent of the time. You
will also know that you have a strategy to use; you will
not be helpless.

As for the 12 per cent, you might try to memorize any
of the words you think you will use frequently. The list to
be memorized will be very small. You can make
memorizing easier by considering the following patterns.

• The *cian* ending is used for a kind of job:

dietician musician politician statistician pediatrician

If you know one, then you know them all.

• The *tian* ending is used for a nationality:

Laotian Egyptian Haitian

(You can remember that it is *ian* by making a link with *Canadian*, where the sound tells you there is an *a*.)

These *sian* endings for nationalities give themselves away by their hard sound:

Asian Malaysian Indonesian

Again, if you know one, then you know them all. One exception is *Russian*, but you would have to be a creative speller to spell it with *tian*. You won't need to worry about *Grecian* – we don't use it much any more, except in an ode by Keats.

• Most words ending in *sion* give themselves away by their hard sound:

evasion lesion division erosion confusion

This is always the case when there is a vowel before the *sion*. Also note: *version, dispersion,* and *aspersion*, which can be pronounced either *shun* or *zhun*. To make a real *shun* or *sion* sound, the word must fall into one of these patterns:

revulsion   pension   session
                 mansion   mission
                              passion

We are not suggesting that patterns like these be listed and learned. We offer them as examples of the kinds of spelling and meaning links that can be made among words. These types of patterns form part of our intrinsic

38

knowledge about words. Often, we are not aware that we have made a generalization about a spelling pattern, but it is this knowledge that enables us to know which words are spelled in similar ways.

Many people make their own generalizations about words that are spelled in a similar way. Those who don't are the ones most likely to make spelling errors. You can help your child make these kinds of links. Whenever you give him or her the spelling of a word, build a list of others which are formed in the same way. Point out what it is that makes them similar. The word lists you build will show you patterns like these:

rarefy	testify	certify	acidify
putrefy	amplify	beautify	calcify
liquefy	clarify	gratify	horrify
stupefy	dignify	falsify	fortify
	glorify	mummify	mystify
	petrify	qualify	rectify
	signify	specify	terrify

If in doubt, which ending would you pick?

By playing the odds, you can use the Las Vegas Rules of Spelling to reduce your chances of making spelling errors, and to give you more confidence in figuring out words.

Teaching the Las Vegas Rules of Spelling

There are three main principles to the Las Vegas Rules:

always   *most of the time*   *never*

39

Here are some examples of the three principles.

Always

• A *kw* sound is spelled *qu*.[1]
(The only exceptions are found in one or two brand names.)
• *Q* is always followed by *u*.
• Every syllable has a vowel or *y*.
• Soft *c* and soft *g* are followed by *i, y,* or *e*.
(*penicillin, cygnet, censorship; prestigious, gyrate, general*)
• When you hear *qu* + short *o*, write *qu* + *a*.
(*squash, quarrel*)
• If a word sounds as if it starts with *f*, and it doesn't, it starts with *ph*.
• If a word sounds as if it ends with *f*, and it doesn't, it ends with *ph*, or more rarely, *gh*.
• Use *dge* after short vowels, and *ge* after long vowels.
(*fudge, cage*)

Most of the Time

• Words do not end in *i*. Use *y*. The ending *ie* is rare.
(*taxi-taxicab; maxi* and *mini* are also abbreviations)
• Occupations end in *er* or *or*.
(not *ar, ur, ir, our* . . . *er* is the most common, for example, *teacher, carpenter; sailor, doctor*)[2]

[1] Note: *choir*.
[2] Some modern *or* endings are fashionable but wrong – *presentor*.

• Use *le* at the ends of words. It is far more common than *el*.

(*fumble, nickel*)

• A *k* sound at the beginning of a word is most likely to be *c*. It is rarely *k*, and even more rarely *ch*.

(*cactus, kerosene, chorus*)

• A *k* sound at the end of a word will not be written *k*. It will be *ck* or *c*.

(*knock, attic*)[1]

• Words ending in *c* will end in *ic* or *iac*.

• *Ary* or *ery*? A place where something is made ends in *ery*.

(*baker-bakery, brewer-brewery*)[2]

• When you hear *chur* at the end of a word, write ture.

(*picture, nature, creature*)

• After a short vowel, put *t* before *ch*.

(*dispatch, ketch, pitch, scotch, crutch*)

The only exceptions are these one-syllable words: *much, such, rich, which*; and these multi-syllable words: *ostrich, duchess, sandwich, attach, bachelor*.

• *Er, or, ar, ur*? If it is a verb, it will end in *er*.

(*deliver, sequester*)[3]

Never

• Never write *shun* at the end of a word.

[1] Note: *trek.*

[2] Note: *factory.*

[3] Note: *favour/favor, savour/savor.*

- No English words end in *j*, *v*, or *q*.[1]
(*judge, rage, live, toque*)
- Never write *kk*. Use *ck* instead.
(*rocker*)
- There are several other letters we never put in pairs.[2]

These, and many more that you can discover, are important spelling concepts which children can learn and practise daily as they write. In this way, they can build up a store of useful information to give them strategies for solving future spelling problems.

Were you wondering about the *shun* words we found? Here they are:

stanchion
eustachian, Appalachian
complexion, crucifixion (plus transfixion, fluxion and
flexion, although flection is
more common)
fashion, cushion
ocean, crustacean
suspicion, coercion
luncheon, truncheon, puncheon

And the four exceptions to the *a-shun* rule:

Dalmatian	Appalachian
crustacean	eustachian

[1] Our motorist friends insist they *rev* their engines. We think this is the only exception, presumably derived from *revolution*.
[2] *Revved* is the only *vv* word we can find.

As a child, one of us made bread in a pancheon. We cannot find this word in a dictionary, and do not know how it is spelled. This is our best guess. We invented this spelling by seeing which of the possibilities looked the most likely.[1] Also, it is probable that *pancheon* is a regional variation of *puncheon*, as both words mean a large, earthenware vessel. This is the kind of logic we all use when we come to spell an unfamiliar word. Usually, we have enough knowledge of patterns, origins, and derivations to come up with the probable spelling – or at least a possible spelling.

We feel certain the spelling *panshun* is impossible.

Handling Homophones

Homophones are words that sound the same but have different spellings and meanings. Here are some examples of words used every day that are frequently misspelled.

where	to	there	here
wear	too	their	hear
ware	two	they're	

We have made the mistake in the past of teaching these words as sets. We have written where, wear, and ware on the board and said to the children, "Never confuse these three words." We have expected them to memorize the spellings along with the meanings. This method has failed.

In order to determine which spelling to use, children

[1] See Visualizing, p. 53

must first place the word in a spelling context. This will give them a pattern they can use – a logical way to figure out the spelling. The homophones listed above are grouped into sound patterns. This is not useful, in fact, it makes spelling more difficult. What makes the words different is not their sound, but their meaning. Therefore, it makes more spelling sense to group them according to meaning:

here
there   *This gives a group of words*
where   *to do with location.*
somewhere
everywhere
nowhere
whereabouts

Once you know the location words, you can easily determine that *hear* and *wear* do not belong in this pattern. You may have to stop and think about it, but you will know you are right. *Ware* is now only used as a suffix, as in *hardware* and *software*, so it falls into a group of its own. If you think of meaning, you will not put *underwear* in this group. You will also have narrowed your options for spelling *their* and *they're* from three to two. Once you are keyed in to thinking of meaning, and if you know about contractions, you can distinguish between these two by trying to put *they are* into your sentence. *Their* is one you have to learn in its own group of sight words:

their   his   your
my   her   our

44

You can put these on a cheat sheet until you can remember them.[1]

Too is one of the most misspelled words in every year of primary school. Children probably read or write it every day, and it is taught and corrected repeatedly, yet they do not learn it. The three spellings of this sound can be taught by first teaching the pattern of the number words:

two
twice
twenty
twins

This will show a reason for the silent *w*. Tell your child that in Scotland the *w* is sounded in *twa*. If you know anyone who is Scottish invite them to demonstrate this pronunciation. Have some fun with a Robert Burns poem or twa.[2] Talk about how language changes over time.

Now you are down to two options instead of three. You can then use a mnemonic trick,[3] for example:

too many, two *o*'s.

Or, you can use a pronunciation cue, for example:

Think of the three bears of the fairy tale. Exaggerate the sound, "the porridge was *tooooo* hot; the chair was *tooooo* big."

[1] See Cheat Sheets, p. 85
[2] Read or sing the Scottish song: Three craws sat upon a wa'. The second verse begins: Twa craws sat upon a wa'.
[3] For more information about mnemonic devices, see p. 63

Even in normal speech, *to* and *too* do not usually sound the same:

I am going *to* school (the *o* is barely sounded).
I was *too* late (the *o* is longer).

Tell your child to listen for the extra *o*.

For homophones such as *right* and *write*, which do not fall into obvious meaning patterns, help your child to make associations by building word families:

right	sight	light	might
bright	fight	tight	plight

For one-syllable words, this is the most common pattern for this sound. Children may then have to learn *write* as an exception, and link it with *wrote*, *written*, and *writing*. One hopes *writing* is a word with which they will be familiar.

Do not bother with *rite*. It is a word the children will not need for some time. Learning to spell should be kept as simple as possible and confined to concepts and words children are likely to use. If you wish, tell them that *rite* is a word, but not one they need to learn now.

One advantage of drawing children's attention to homophones and their problems is that they become aware of high-risk words. They can look out for them when they are proof-reading, and check that they have used the right spelling.

There are two good principles to remember when teaching homophones.

1. Group words together because the spelling is similar, for example, *here, there,* and *where.* Never group words because they are different, for example, *where, wear,* and *ware.*

2. Teach one homophone at a time along with its group of similar words. Do not try to teach two or three alternate spellings at the same time.

Patterns and Generalizations

The more patterns you know and the more able you are to make generalizations, the better speller you will be. We are not always aware of it, but we apply our knowledge of patterns constantly as we write.

Knowing a pattern or word family can be useful to children as they try to spell. While it is possible and often necessary to memorize single words, especially those we use frequently, it can be far more productive to teach spelling patterns that can be applied to many words.

Many of the generalizations we have made about spelling are subconscious. Often, we are only aware that some letter combinations look right and others do not. Can you think of a word in which a double vowel is followed by a double consonant?[1] Probably not. If you tried to put this combination in a word, it would look wrong. This is a generalization you have made about spelling.

It is not possible to teach every pattern or to be aware

[1] In England, you would find *woollen*: in North America, it is written *woolen.*

47

of every possible spelling generalization. This does not matter. The knowledge that patterns do exist, that spelling is not random and illogical, can give power to young and struggling spellers. When they come to an unfamiliar word, they will not have to make wild guesses or choose a simpler word; they will try to make the links that make spelling possible. If they come up with the wrong result, they will know that they have alternate strategies to use.

A pattern[1] can be presented as a list of words that share a common spelling element; it tells you what combinations of letters are possible. A generalization[2] is something each person must make independently. A generalization is the knowledge that tells you that a word you want to spell is similar to several others you know and probably follows the same pattern. It tells you what is likely. Collecting word families and grouping words can draw children's attention to patterns. Once they have made the appropriate generalization, children will be able to apply it to new words in the future.

As often as possible, get children to make links among words.

• Try not to teach words singly. If you write a word for a child, always try to write two or three others that fit the same pattern. Ask the child to generate more words for the list.
• If your child asks how to spell a word, try to help him or her determine the spelling by suggesting other words that might share spelling elements. Ask questions: Do you

[1] For example, *play, lay, may, clay, tray, say.*
[2] For example, a long *a* sound at the end of words is often spelled *ay.*

know any other words which have the same sound? Do you know any other similar words? What other words do you know that might be linked in meaning? Even if the child cannot arrive at the correct spelling, you will be teaching a strategy for figuring out words.

• Work with your child to sort and classify words according to spelling patterns. Ask them to justify the ways they have sorted. This justification is often a spelling generalization, for example, "I put these together because they all have double consonants."

• Use correct spelling terminology, such as "consonant" and "long/short vowel." Terminology is not difficult to learn when used in the context of talking about language. Knowing these words will enable you to talk about parts of words.

• Talk through your own spelling processes as you write, for example, "I always remember the *c* in *medicine* because it goes with *medical*."

Pronunciation Cues

Sometimes letters appear in words to help in pronunciation. Consider the following rule:

i and *e* soften *c* and *g*

This gives us words like:

*ci*vil   *ce*nt
presti*gi*ous   *ge*neral

This also tells us that any other vowel following *c* or *g* will give a hard consonant:

*ca*t	*cucu*mber	*co*d
*ga*in	*gu*llible	*go*pher

This can help when we are adding endings. As an example: if you follow the regular rule for adding *ing* to *picnic*, you would get *picnicing*. This would be pronounced *picnissing*, therefore we have to add a *k* – *picnicking*, *trafficking*, *mimicking*, and *politicking*.

Another example: if you added an *ous* ending to *courage*, following the usual rule, you would have *couragous*. This would have to be pronounced with a hard *g*, so we do not drop the *e*.

courageous, outrageous
but   raging and aging are correct

If we remember what *i* and *e* do to pronunciation, we can avoid numerous common spelling errors.

The best way to learn this kind of spelling generalization is by collecting words and putting them into categories, for example:

noticeable   replaceable   serviceable   knowledgeable

Origins and Derivations

Engage your child's interest in spellings by telling them about word origins.

•Numerous words have come from people's names:

Louis Braille	Rudolf Diesel	Nicholas Chauvin
Samuel Maverick	Friedrich Mesmer	Teddy Roosevelt
Amelia Bloomer	Charles Boycott	Ambrose E
Louis Pasteur	Andre Ampere	Burnside
Robert Bunsen	James Watt	Saint Audrey[1]

• You will never know how close you came to eating a peanut butter Montague. If you want to know why, find out about the origin of the sandwich.

• Many words have come into English from other languages. Here are a few examples:

from Native American	raughroughoun (raccoon)	isquontersquashe (squash)
from Inuit	kayak	
from Norse	knife	hut
from Latin	exit	fan (fanaticus)
from Hindu	pyjama	gymkhana
from Greek	atomic	drama
from Malay	gingham	ketchup
from Chinese	tea	mandarin
from Japanese	kimono	typhoon
from Portuguese	banana	molasses
from Arabic	algebra	zero
from Gaelic	slogan	clan
from Spanish	rodeo	mosquito
from Hebrew	camel	cinnamon
from Dutch	wagon	yacht

[1] These last three gave us the following words: *teddy bear*, *sideburns*, and *tawdry*, used to describe lace sold at her fair.

from German	kindergarten	sauerkraut
from Italian	umbrella	piano
from Russian	sputnik	glasnost
from Iranian	shawl	sandal

• French was introduced to England after the Norman conquest in 1066. For several generations after that, French was the language of the ruling class, English that of the servant and peasant class.[1] Hence, our alternate names for cooked and raw meat: the lord, who saw the meat cooked, used the French word, while the servantfarmer, who saw it raw, used the English word.

cow	beef/boeuf
sheep	mutton/mouton
pig	pork/porc

Words used in everyday life tended to be English, for example, *man, day, drink, sleep, love, water*, while the words of government, leisure, and the law tended to be French: *parliament, justice, pleasure, castle, chivalry.*

• Many words came from the names of places:

| Cologne | Kashmir | Frankfurt | Tabasco |
| Hamburg | Manila | Tangier | Nimes[2] |

• Lewis Carroll, in *Through the Looking Glass*, started the custom of making portmanteau words, by combining two existing words. Now we have words like these:

[1] Latin was the language of the church.

[2] Serge de Nimes = denim

glimmer	(glare + shimmer)
medicare	(medical + care)
flare	(flame + glare)
twirl	(twist + swirl)

• We have acronyms, words created from initials:

radar   sonar   scuba   cobol[1]

• Computer science has introduced new vocabulary. We now *access information*, *interface* with one another, and want things to be *user-friendly*.

Not only is this kind of information interesting, it helps us make first meaning, and then spelling links.

Visualizing

A stratagem many people use when trying to figure out how to spell a word is to write it two or more ways and see which looks best. If we have a reasonably good sense of what is possible, this can help to eliminate the incorrect spelling. Do not assume that your child will automatically do this; she or he may think that looking a word up in a dictionary is the only legitimate way to check spelling. Teach him or her that this stratagem is often practised by adults. If children can select the right spelling from the

[1] Radio Detection And Ranging
  Sound Navigation and Ranging
  Self Contained Underwater Breathing Apparatus
  Common Business Oriented Language

alternatives they have written, they develop more confidence in their own spelling knowledge.

Using the Dictionary

How many times have we heard the plea, "How can I look up a word if I don't know how to spell it?" We use a dictionary for two main purposes: to check the spelling of a word, and to find out what a word means. In both instances, the spelling of a word helps us locate it. It would seem that for poor spellers, a dictionary is less than useful. Not so.

Finding Your Way Around the Dictionary

Finding a word in a dictionary requires two pieces of information:

a knowledge of alphabetical order;
the first few letters of the word (at least).

Alphabetical order is easy to teach; there are plenty of rhymes and alphabet picture books. Many of us have learned to say it backwards, a useful trick for dictionary searching. You can almost make a rhyme of it:
Z Y X and W V,
U T S and R Q P
O N M and L K J
I H G
F E D
C B A.

(We did say almost.)

If you watch young children searching for a word in a dictionary, you will notice they often read in the same way they read other books – they start at the beginning and keep going until they find what they are looking for. This method does not work well for reference material. Children need to know that all reading is not the same; they cannot always work in chronological order. Children need a sense of location of letters within the alphabet. Teach them some basic search skills.

• Say a letter, and challenge your child to open the dictionary at that letter. How close can she or he come? Let your child challenge you in return. If you have two or more children in the house at the time, let them challenge each other.
• Try to open a dictionary at the page where your name would appear. Practise this with your child, for each name you have. Opening the dictionary at your name page can give a baseline, from which you can search either forwards or backwards.
• Some larger and more expensive dictionaries have indented tabs to show where letters begin. Try to have at least one of these dictionaries in your home. Your child can get used to locating the initial letter, before trying to find the whole word.
• Show your child how to use the guide words. Give a word, then ask him or her to find not the word, but the page it is on.
• Make dictionary usage a normal part of everyday life. The more familiar a dictionary becomes, the easier it will

be to use.

• Have available as many different dictionaries as you can. Children should know that not all dictionaries provide the same service: on some occasions a pocket version is sufficient, while on other occasions, they will need a comprehensive dictionary.

Search skills are important. If it takes too long to find a word, the children will not find the dictionary useful.

How to Look Up a Word You Cannot Spell

The first principle is a "most of the time" rule. Consonant sounds tend to be reliable; if a word sounds as if it starts with *t*, chances are it starts with *t*.

If this rule lets you down when you go to the dictionary, it is necessary to use an alternate stratagem. This involves knowing what the possible alternatives are, and where you should look first:

• If it sounds as if it starts with *f*, and it doesn't, it will start with *ph*.
• If it sounds as if it starts with *n*, and it doesn't, try *kn* (the most likely alternative), then try *gn* (much rarer), then try *pn* (these are all scientific or medical, and all start with *pneu*), and, as a last resort, try *mn* (*mnemonic* is the only one in our dictionary; use *memory* and *amnesia* as cues).
• If it sounds as if it starts with *k*, and it doesn't, try *c* (most common). Then try *ch* (rare).
• If it sounds like *kw*, try *qu*.
• If it sounds as if it starts with *j*, and it doesn't, try *g*.

• If it sounds as if it starts with *r*, and it doesn't, try *wr*.

• If it sounds as if it starts with *s*, and it doesn't, try *ps* (*pseudo, psycho, psalm*).

• If it sounds as if it starts with *t*, and it doesn't, try *p* (most of us will never encounter this, unless we have an interest in exotic beasts).[1]

• If it sounds as if it starts with *o*, and it doesn't, try *h*.

• If it sounds as if it starts with a particular vowel, and it doesn't, try all the other vowels until you find it. Vowels are often unpredictable.

Also remember:

• *Q* is always followed by *u*.

• *W* is often followed by *h*.

• Many vowel sounds can be represented by different combinations of vowels. You may have to hunt around.

A few basic alternatives like these will allow you to find your way around a dictionary. The more skilled you become at knowing alternatives, the less time it will take you to find a word. Until you can remember these tips, you might keep a cheat sheet inside your dictionary as reference. It should tell you what the possible alternatives are, and in which order you should try them. It might look like this.

F	PH			
J	G			
K	C	CH	QU	
N	KN	GN	PN	MN

[1] Like *Pteradons* and *ptarmigans*.

R	WR	RH
S	PS	
T	PT	
O	HO	
Q	+U	
W	+H	

Most unpredictable and silent groups of letters, such as *ght*, come later in a word. As children learn more about these patterns of spelling, they will be able to find words more quickly. Until that time, knowing the first part of a word will help get them started.

Proof-reading

When we were in school, the teacher was the copy editor, proof-reading our writing as part of the marking process. We had no chance to do our own proof-reading because for us writing was a one-shot operation; everything was supposed to come out right the first time. Once the teacher had isolated all the errors, we were expected to do the corrections. This was seen as a disgrace and a punishment; little learning was attached to the correction process. The most obvious lesson was that the less we wrote, and the simpler the words we used, the fewer mistakes we were likely to make. This lesson did not make better writers, nor better spellers.

Rather than perpetuating this system, we want to teach our children that editing and proof-reading are the final and necessary steps in the writing process. We teach them the *why* of proof-reading by providing many opportunities for them to share and display their writing. We teach them the *when* of proof-reading by focusing on editing only when composition and organization are complete. Let us now look at the *how* of proof-reading.

We know that even good spellers sometimes read through their work and do not spot all the spelling mistakes. You may have already spotted a proof-reading slip in this book; it is difficult and time-consuming to be perfect. Readers are constantly predicting what ideas, information, or words will come next as they look for meaning in the text. A reader does not need to look too closely at much of the visual information on the page; much of it can be taken as understood. This is one reason why fluent readers do not always learn about spelling as they read – they move quickly to meanings, and do not notice the details of letters and words. This is also why good readers and spellers can sometimes make poor proof-readers.

On the other hand, it is not possible to be a good proof-reader without looking at the meaning and language the writer is trying to convey. A proof-reader often needs to consider the meaning, the part of speech, the tense and so on, to know if a word is spelled correctly. You cannot proof-read by reading a text backwards and looking at the words one at a time. Proof-reading has its own group of skills which need to be practised.

You can help your children become better proof-readers. Here are several strategems you can suggest.

• Look *for*, rather than *at*. Do not just read over the writing – look for specific things. Your own experience will gradually teach you what kinds of errors to look for.

• Know which words cause trouble for you, and look out for them. Build your own cheat sheet as a reference for these words.

• Recognize homophones and give them some extra thought. As an example, if you have written *there*, make sure that the spelling is correct.

• Offer your help as a proof-reader for a friend. You do not need to be an expert speller to do this. Perhaps all you need to say is, "Are you sure about this word?"

• Proof-read only when all composition and organization is complete. Then you can focus on spelling.

• Even if you cannot find every error, do the best you can. Ask for help with the others. You will get more proficient as you go along.

Spelling Trivia

Some of Noah Webster's "improved" spellings, which were later taken out of his dictionary, included: *bilt, tung, breth, helth, iz, relm, beleeve, mashine, wimmin,* and *yeer.*

• *Poodle* and *puddle* have the same origin. *Poodle* comes from the German word *pudelhund,* meaning "splash dog."

• Would you mark these words as spelling errors?

astroid crysal galop orchestia tecnology warehous windrow

They are not misspellings, but are all real words:

– an adjective meaning "star-shaped"
– part of an archery bow
– a 19th-century German dance
– a genus of crustacean

– the study of children
– fishes, the plural of "warehou"
– a row of hay raked together to dry.

• *Daffodil* comes into English from Dutch, which is hardly surprising, as the Netherlands is famous for bulbs. What may be surprising is that our meaning of daffodil is the result of a mistake. *Affodil* is derived from the Greek *Asphodel*, meaning "flower."

• *Caterpillar* comes from two Latin words, *catta* and *pilosus*, meaning "hairy cat."

• Word meanings often change over time:
– *girl* and *niece* used to refer to either a boy or girl.
– *pipe* used to mean any musical instrument.
– *to starve* meant to die.
– *lumber* used to mean a room for wood.
– *meat* used to mean any food.
– *bible* used to mean any book.

• Sports fans may be interested in these origins:
– *racket*, from the Arabic *rahat*, meaning "palm of the hand."
– *score*, from the Old Norse word, *notch*. Scores were kept by making notches in wood. We retain this meaning when we use *score* when referring to marking lines in wood or paper.
– *arena*, from the Latin *harena*, meaning "sand."

• We have adopted words from Greek myths, for example, *Atlas*, *Nemesis*, *Tantalus*, and *Achilles*.

If you find this kind of word trivia interesting, you have something in common with most people. Background knowledge gives colour and meaning to our language.

Most of us enjoy playing with words, whether through board games, circle games, crossword puzzles, or puns. Much of our humour is founded on the ambiguity and flexibility of words. Words have their own fascination, and the more you know, the more interesting they become. Also, the more you know about words, the better you will be able to make the connections necessary for spelling them correctly.

Spelling need not only be seen as a by-product of writing. The study of words as entities in themselves is a valid and interesting subject for study.

How to Remember

Study Skills

If there is a particular word your child needs to memorize, you might suggest some or all of the following:

• Print the word and keep it in a handy place to refer to whenever you need it. Repeated use will help memorization.
• Several times a day, try to write the word from memory, then check and see if you were right.
• Note which parts of the word you misspell, and concentrate on these. Feel good about the number of letters you do get in the right place.
• Look at the word for 15 to 30 seconds. Close your eyes gently so you can continue to "see" the word. Then write the word and see if you were right.
• Invent a way to pronounce the word that will help you

with spelling, for example, say *Wed nes day*, in order to remember all the letters, and *ne k essary* to remember the order of *c* and ss in *necessary*.

• Print words you are trying to visualize, rather than writing them in script. Printed letters are more distinctive, and stand out as individuals. Young children often prefer to work with uppercase letters as they are distinct from one another. *B* and *D* are easier to distinguish between than are *b* and *d*.

• When you find a method that helps you, share it. Talking about the method will help you, and perhaps your listener too.

Mnemonic Devices

A mnemonic device is a trigger that makes a link between words and spellings and can help one remember seemingly illogical and random spellings.

The best mnemonic device is one you think up for yourself, one that has a significant meaning that will come to mind when you need it. It may be as personal as remembering that *phone* starts like *Phenix*; this would not be useful for most people, but can be infallible for a few of us.

Sometimes we adopt another person's mnemonic trigger if we find it memorable. Share any tricks or secrets you have, however illogical and strange they sound. Ask your child to share his or hers with you. It is not profitable, however, to ask children to memorize the tricks. The whole point of a mnemonic device is that you think of it instantly when it is needed. If the mnemonic device cannot be remembered easily, it will not be useful.

Here are some examples of mnemonics which have worked for some people:

> Hear clearly with your ears.
> U and I build a house.
> I'll be your friend 'til the end.
> Age is advantageous.
> A beach is by the sea: a beech is a tree.
> A piece of pie.
> The principal is your pal.
> I like my juice with ice.

What Not to Learn

We no longer consider it possible in our schools to make a list of all the facts a person needs to know to be considered educated. We probably never could, but we tried anyway. Today, we are more concerned with teaching problem-solving strategies so children will be able to cope with whatever situations they will meet in their worlds. We teach children how to find the information they need, rather than relying on rote learning. What is important is *to know what to do with information, how to use it to solve problems as they arise.*

In teaching spelling, we have come to recognize that rote learning of a few selected words does not enable children to solve future spelling problems. Even if it were possible for all children to memorize the 3000 most commonly used words, these would represent only a fraction of the words they will use in their writing. We know, too, that many children cannot memorize all the words on a list, while others can only remember the words for as long as it takes to do the test. It is the application of spelling knowledge to new words that is the useful skill. Knowing how spelling works, how to proof-read, and how to use a dictionary are more important spelling skills than a few memorized words.

We know that rote memorization is the most difficult way to learn anything, the most boring, and the least motivating. Moreover, it often produces learning that is short-lived. Things we have learned by rote are only retained by the memory if they are important to us, if they are used constantly, or if they have engaged our interest for some reason. We remember facts like the alphabet and our telephone numbers because we use the information regularly. We remember other people's phone numbers if we call them frequently enough. Have you noticed, though, that when you move, you quickly forget the phone number you have remembered and used for years? We remember favourite poems and songs from our childhood, but the poems we were assigned to memorize did not stay with us for long.

Children will learn many words by memorizing them. They learned to write their own names in this way, first by copying them and then by repeating them so many times that the spelling became automatic. When your children were starting to write they learned some sight words because they saw them and wrote them repeatedly, words like *the* and *my*. They learned these words because they needed them; they remembered them because they used them and so re-memorized them constantly. Words that are useful for us or have significance in our lives are likely to be remembered.

Many words can be learned only by memorization. Many of the most commonly used words fall into this category, words like *why*, *because*, and *eight*. Since these words will be used over and over again, it is worthwhile spending time to learn them. Because we use them repeatedly, there is a good chance that they will pass into long-term memory and become automatic for us. However, if at any time we cease to use them, they may, like our old telephone numbers, fade from our minds.

Because rote learning is so difficult and transitory, we should use it as little as possible. Fortunately in spelling, we have other methods to help us remember words.

Most words fall at least in part into some kind of group. Even *because* has three predictable consonants and an easy-to-spell first syllable. If we think of the meaning and derivation – be the cause – this may also help the spelling. Few words need to be learned in total isolation from other words. Whenever possible, words should be linked together in their natural spelling patterns. Learning about one word can give information about many other words.

4. Helping Your Child to Be a Better Speller

Understanding Spelling Development

The way children learn to spell is much like the way they learned to talk. They start by imitating what they see the people around them doing, gradually coming closer to using standard forms.

When young children are learning to spell, they tend to show their learning by a particular sequence. This is what it looks like.

Example 1

• They print a series of random letters.

ISKMiBHCSbFA
I   was   at   church   learning
about   God

Example 2

• They print one consonant to represent each word. It is usually the first sound of the word.

What starts with the letter A

At this point, your child will be trying to make connections between letters and sounds, and this is a good time to give all kinds of practice at working with different sounds. You can play games like "I spy with my little eye, something in this room beginning with *b* like *ball*. Your child asks, "Is it a balloon?" You reply, "No but balloon begins like ball." Your child asks, "Is it a table?" You reply, "No, and table does not begin like ball." There are many other sound games you can play, which will help your child to internalize sounds related to words.

Example 3

• They begin to print a final letter, as well as an initial letter. At this point, they begin to put spaces between the words.

When this thing
happened it was like
I fell down on the side walk

WN eS FS TOO
HPN eTWS LKes
I FOON TS S WCK

Try to be as encouraging as possible at this stage, as this is hard work for a young child.

Example 4

• All syllables and sounds in words are represented by letters.

I eOT a LiTTi HCickee
I QcsdIT/99 OiT a LITToMar
thanIwos saPosto

I got a little chickee.
I accidently ate a little too
much than I was supposed to

6 yr. 2 mo.

At this stage, children know enough about how spelling works to begin to build a repertoire of spelling patterns, and add to their store of sight words.

This experience of building words on the basis of letter sounds teaches children a basic spelling concept: words are not memorized but constructed using the best available information.

When children have reached a stage where they are close to standard spelling, they can begin to learn the many patterns and generalizations which enable us to be good spellers. Because there are so many patterns to learn, it will take a number of years before they have enough experience and knowledge to be accurate spellers. While they are learning, we must accept that there is much young children have not had a chance to learn, and help them believe that eventually they will become spellers.

Reinforcing Spelling Concepts

Collections

Once children are aware that two or three words may work in the same way, they can begin collections. Collecting words helps children form generalizations about how words are spelled. Learning words in groups can help children link words together to remember spellings. Knowing that by learning one word you can now spell many other words gives a sense of power and control over the many alternatives to spelling.

Here are some examples to show you how you can use collections to raise spelling awareness.

• Suppose your child has been reading or reciting, "Humpty Dumpty." Ask, "Which word rhymes with *wall*?" Print the word *fall*. Then ask your child to suggest other words she or he knows which rhyme with *wall*. You could leave the list up for a few days, so that your child can add more rhyming words as she or he finds them in his or her reading. Children who know the initial consonants you have used will be able to read the words on the list. Very soon, even young children will be able to work with you to make their own lists of words which follow a pattern. Sometimes, your child will suggest a word that sounds as if it fits the pattern, but is spelled differently. As an example, your child might suggest *doll*. You can then say that this word doesn't fit the pattern. Write it off to one side by itself. In some cases, this can be the start of a whole new pattern.

• Ask your child to tell you words that have the *ee* sound, as in *feet*. Print the words on a large piece of paper some will have *ee*, some will have *ea*, some will have *ei*. When you have listed all the words ask what is different about them. Cut out the words on the list with your child and categorize them. You can then print new lists, showing the different patterns of the *ee* sound. Each list could then be saved and used as a reference.

• When you generate lists of words that follow a pattern, they will often include words that are an exception to the pattern. Encourage your child to discover these words. If your child is unsure, check the spelling together.

• Your child will learn that if a word sounds as if it starts with *n*, and it doesn't, there are several possibilities. If they are going to look the word up in the dictionary, children don't want to waste time. Will they try first *kn*, *gn*, or *pn*? First, ask them to predict which one they think is the most likely. Then ask them to make a list of all the words they can think of for each. They, and you, may be surprised.[1]

• Children can work alone or with you to find derivational patterns. These might be words sharing the same prefix or the same meaning base, for example: the *uni* words (*uniform*, *unicycle*, *unicorn*) or the *two* words (*two*, *twins*, *twenty*, *twice*).

Classification

Classification is an activity that draws attention to patterns and generalizations. Whenever children learn a new word or spelling pattern, it is a good idea to link it with other words which share the same pattern. Here are some examples of activities that help children to classify words.

• Together, with your child, generate a list of words which begin with the hard *c* sound. Then list them according to the beginning letter, *c* or *k*. First predict which list you think will be longer. For each word you think of, your child could predict the spelling, check it, and put the word in the appropriate column. The final list will give useful information about spelling.[2]

---

[1] For more about dictionary alternatives, see p. 55.

[2] Most of the time, use *c*. Use *k* only when followed by *i* or *e*. Remember that *i* and *e* soften *c* and *g*. Don't worry about *kleptomaniac*.

72

• Give your child a number of words to classify in as many ways as possible, for example, number of letters, beginning sounds, number of syllables, and meanings. Ask your child to explain and justify the groups. This kind of categorization forces children to examine words and to look for patterns and similarities. The best way to categorize or classify words is to cut them out and physically move them around. This not only helps the visual learner, it saves a lot of time. After a classification activity, you can ask your child to summarize what she or he has discovered about spelling.

Exploration

Most people find a certain fascination in words. True investigation comes when children reflect on why some words are harder to spell than others, how our language developed, and why some games and puzzles present more problems than others. Is it the number of letters? The number of vowels? Do some letters make it harder than other letters? It is always good to hold a discussion after a word game. You will find a lot of spontaneous ideas and arguing during the games as your child asks questions and justifies decisions.

It is this kind of word investigation that leads to spelling awareness. The way in which children go about finding solutions can be more valuable learning than the answers they find. While they may forget individual words, children are more likely to remember strategies for discovery. This is the kind of knowledge they can use in the future to solve spelling problems.

Games and Puzzles

Parents who have taken children on long car trips know all about the fascination of word games. Here are a few you can use when your family is together.

I Packed My Bag

This is a circle game, best played in a small group of two to five people. The first person starts by saying, "I packed my bag, and in it I put an apple" (something starting with *a*). The second person continues by repeating the first item, and adding one starting with *b*, "I packed my bag, and in it I put an apple and a beaver." The game works best when the players help each other out when the string of words starts to get long. You can make this a co-operative game by getting everyone to repeat the list each time, allowing the next player in turn to add a word. In this way, everyone participates all the time.

Word String

This is also a circle game for a small group. The first person says a word, the second person follows with a word starting with the last letter of the previous word, for example ba*ll*, *l*io*n*, *n*e*w*, *w*indow. No repetitions are allowed. The idea is to make a long string of words. They can be written down. Players soon get to know which letters are more difficult to start words with, and start planning ahead to catch the next person out.

You can make the game more advanced by introducing a theme, for example, the words must all be animals, countries, or a type of food.

Beetle

This used to be called "Hangman," but as the concept isn't pleasant, we've renamed it. This is a game for two players. One thinks of a word and writes down a dash for each letter in the word. The other player then has to figure out the word by suggesting one letter at a time. Only one guess at the complete word is allowed. If the suggested letter is not in the word, a part of the beetle is drawn. The finished beetle looks like this:

It will have three body parts, six legs, and two antennae. This allows for eleven guesses to fill in letters.

Children quickly learn which are the most commonly used vowels and consonants, and which go together in combinations. This is a particularly good game for older children. They learn that once you have any letters in a word, options for other letters are dramatically reduced. The more letters there are, the easier the prediction becomes, until there is only one possible answer. The game is excellent for teaching possible and probable letter sequences.

Concentration

This is an individual game. One person chooses a word, and discovers how many other words can be made from the letters, for example, fourteen- and fifteen-year-old students in Cookstown, Ontario, came up with 180 words from *Saskatchewan*. A variation is to print the word on a large piece of paper and put it on the fridge door for a few days. Your children can then add words as they discover them.

Word Hunt

This game involves a problem that must be solved by finding words, for example:

• Write words with two *a*'s, three *a*'s, four *a*'s (try this with any letter).
• Write words with four *a*'s, four *e*'s, four *i*'s, and so on.
• Find words that have all the vowels in them. Try words that have all the vowels in alphabetical order.[1]
• Write words that have no vowels in them (use *y*). What is the longest word you can find with no vowels except *y*?
• Write as many words as you can that contain double

---

[1] *Facetiously* and *abstemiously* have all six vowels in alphabetical order.

vowels – *aa*, *ee*, *ii*, *oo*, *uu* (children will discover which are most common/rare).

• For each consonant, try to write a word that has the consonant doubled (some will never double, others will double only in compound words, for example, *fishheads*).

• How many ways can you find to pronounce the name, *Mr Hough*? Write a rhyming word to demonstrate each pronunciation.[1]

• Which word ending is the most common: *eat* or *ate*?

Word Frame

Give your child a word frame, as in the examples below.

r _ _ d   m_ _t   d_ _r

Ask your child to fill in the frame with as many words as possible. Encourage the use of a dictionary, if your child finds this helpful. The purpose of this game is to draw your child's attention to vowels used in combination, and those that are not used in combination.

Word Middles

This is a variation on the word frame. Give your child a group of letters which could be found inside a word, for example, *eat*. They must then write as many words as they can with these letters inside, for example, *meat, creation, feature, defeat*.

[1] For example, Mr. Hoff as in cough.

Consonant-Vowel Clues

In this game, you would give your child clues, giving only consonants and the number of vowels.

- a vegetable that grows underground: *n, n,* and three vowels
- a continent: *r, p,* and four vowels
- an open space: *r,* and three vowels
- a province: *n, t, r,* and four vowels[1]

If that is not enough, you will have to give further clues. As your child begins to understand this game, she or he can be the one who invents the questions to try to stump you.

Crosswords

Crossword puzzles are one of the best ways to explore spelling. As letters of a word fill in, leaving blank spaces between, the possibilities for the missing letters decrease. This can help the children to think of possible and impossible letter groupings. As an example, you have the following:

_ _ _ _ _ _ _ _

You have no information, most initial letters are possible, but you fill in the *t.*

[1] Onion, Europe, area, Ontario.

_ t _ _ _ _ _ _

Only a limited number of letters can start the word, and only a limited number can follow the *t*.

The word must start with *s* or a vowel (keep *p* in mind just in case).

If you have these letters filled in

_ t _ p _ a _ e

you can work out that:

• only a consonant can come between the *a* and *e*.
• only a consonant can start the word, as a vowel would require a double *t*, and this could not be followed by *p*.
• the word must start with *s*.

s t _ p _ a _ e

• only a vowel can follow the *t*.
• there is a very good chance that the letter following the *p* is another *p*.[1]

This is the type of reasoning that goes through one's mind while solving a crossword puzzle. You can help children to figure out the logic of words by working through and discussing a few crosswords. Another option is to have your child work with a friend or two. Group work builds in talk and negotiation, and the children can learn from one another.

[1] The word is stoppage.

Commercial Games

Games like Scrabble and Lexicon are useful additions to your spelling sessions. Any game that requires participants to manipulate letters and words is likely to build word awareness and spelling knowledge.

Working As a Tutor

Here are a few suggestions to help you as you work with your child.

Show Them How

• For a very young child who has not yet begun to attempt writing, you might print as she or he dictates. This models the act of writing, and demonstrates that writing preserves your language and message.
• Demonstrate letter shapes for a child who has not yet learned them.
• For beginner spellers, draw their attention to initial consonants in books. Ask them to suggest other words that start with the same sound.
• Provide spellings of a few specific words your child needs.
• Talk about how you work out spellings when you write, for example: "This *kw* sound is always spelled *qu. Quiet* starts like *queen* and *quick.*" "I remember to put *ery* on *stationery* because I think of the *er* in *paper.*"
• "Talk through" the spelling as you make suggestions,

for example, "*Shave* starts with the same sound as your name. What are the two letters you should use?"

"This is spelled *sigh*. You could think of it along with *sight* and *night*. Do you know of any others that might be the same?"

"This is the name of a place. It needs a capital letter."

• Talk about what you are doing when your child is watching you write: "These are called 'periods'. They show when I am ending one sentence, and starting another. Where do you think the next one should go?"

• Choose a word from a reading experience, and use it as a model to teach a spelling concept or pattern, for example: "*Jumped* sounds as if it ends in *t*, but it doesn't. It is always *ed*. Let's make a list of words we know with this ending."

Help with Proof-reading

• Suggest words or concepts to proof-read for. If there are some common words your child constantly misspells, write them down or help your child start a "cheat sheet" as a reference. Use the pages at the back of this book. Next time, ask your child to proof-read for those words.

• If your child is having difficulty with proof-reading, mark the beginning of lines that contain errors, and ask him or her to find and correct the errors.

Promote Confidence

If your child is worried about spelling, take opportunities

to point out correct spellings and areas of progress. Set realistic proof-reading and correcting goals for your child so the task does not become overwhelming.

The Personalized Dictionary

The dictionary is such a basic tool of spelling that all older children should have one of their own. It can be a workbook, as well as a reference book. It should be large enough to have a good range of words, and have enough white space in which to make notes and notations. The dictionary may be used well if you instruct your child about the following points.

• Make a mark beside a word that you look up for spelling. It might be a dot or the date. If you come to look the same word up again, make another mark. You will soon get to know which words give you trouble. Words you need to look up regularly are words worth learning.
• A dictionary usually provides derivations and origins of words. This information can be useful in learning the spelling, as well as the meaning. Looking up one word can help you to spell a group of related words.
• Dictionaries also give information on pronunciation. Pronouncing all parts of a word correctly can help in spelling. It is worthwhile to learn how to read the pronunciation cues. Practise articulating words correctly.
• If you look up a word with a prefix, you will usually find a long list of other words which use the same prefix. Knowing the meaning and the spelling can help spell these other words. This kind of "many for the price of

one" learning can give spelling confidence.

• When you look up a word in a dictionary, you usually read several other words on the same page. This can spark an interest in new and unusual words and broaden your vocabulary. You might find a word you can try to use during the course of the day.

One word of caution about dictionaries. If they are used extensively during first-draft writing, they can hinder the flow of composition. A child who goes to the dictionary frequently in the early stages of writing is a child who is afraid of making a spelling mistake. Young children often give themselves away when they constantly ask, "How do you spell_____?"

If you see this kind of over-dependence on correct spelling on first-draft writing, encourage your child to make his or her best attempt at the word, perhaps making a note to check the spelling at a convenient time.

Computer-Assisted Spelling

Some people think that if children use a computer to check spelling, they are somehow cheating. What they don't realize is that most spell-check programs ask children to select the correct word from a list of other words that look alike. This is a fine type of visual discrimination, and is vital in the development of any good speller.

A simple word-processing program can help beginning spellers to write. For these children, finding a letter on a keyboard can be faster than printing it with a pencil. Also, recognizing a *B* is much easier than remembering how to make one. Young children who have little control over wandering fingers can produce writing that looks perfect to them. This can be highly motivating for a beginner. With only a little learning about letter sounds, the children can produce text that both of you can read. As children write, read, and learn more about the patterns of spelling, their ability to spell and print will grow.

Many older children come to see themselves as poor spellers, subsequently drawing the conclusion that they are poor writers. Producing a final draft can be such drudgery that they never want to finish anything. Many children are not risk-takers: even if they are not poor spellers, they are so afraid of making spelling errors that they write as little as possible to diminish their chances of making a mistake. Others are not willing to take spelling risks, and will always write *big* and never try *enormous*. Writing less will not help them learn to spell, and it certainly will not make them better writers.

For these children, using a computer spell-checker can free them from worrying about spelling mistakes. They can focus on their compositions, use their most adventurous language, and know that spelling errors can be corrected without undue hardship.

Also, the children can learn about the place and relative importance of spelling in the writing process. We must again apply the real-world rules of spelling: for a published book, a billboard, or a business letter, what matters is not *who* fixed up the spelling or *how* it was done. What matters is that it *was* done.

Computer spell-checkers do not do all the work for

you. They will not correct your spelling, nor can they tell when you have used a wrong homophone. What most will do is proof-read for, and draw your attention to, impossible spellings, before offering alternative spellings. Many have a phonetic input function, before offering suggested alternative spellings. Ultimately, the writer must decide on the basis of his or her own spelling knowledge.

An acceptance of the principle that we will give children all the help they need to come up with correct spelling easily does not mean that we do not expect them to learn how to do it for themselves. It is a recognition that there is a lot to learn to become a proficient speller, and it is a long process. In the interim, the worst thing that can happen is that a child stops writing. When this happens, learning about spelling, not to mention writing, is no longer possible. Just as we lived happily through the babbling when the young child was learning to talk, so we must live patiently through the years of invented and inaccurate spelling while we give the child time to build up a knowledge of standard forms. However, you need to be there, to help and support your child along the way.

Cheat Sheets

"Cheat Sheet" is one of the many terms we have adopted from the world of computers. A cheat sheet is a list of facts and information one expects to use often. Our computer manual provides one – a one-page list of the most-needed commands. The purpose of a cheat sheet is to save time checking larger reference sources for facts and information you have not memorized or learned yet.

What usually happens is that once you have looked something up a few times, you remember it and no longer need the cheat sheet. This makes it a doubly useful tool for teaching spelling.

• Children can make a list of words they wish to refer to. It might be words they know they have trouble spelling or words they will need for a particular theme or topic. They can easily refer to the list when they are writing, or better still, when they are proof-reading. It is quicker and less distracting than using a dictionary.

• After looking up a word several times on the cheat sheet and correcting it in the writing, a child may remember it without looking. Children can also be encouraged to try the word first, then check to see if they are right. When they know the word, it can be taken off the cheat sheet.

Children can make their own cheat sheets for special topics or for their own problem words. You can suggest words they are having trouble with. You can also provide cheat sheets for commonly used words, such as days and months, theme words, and service words such as *who*, *the*, *what*, *because*. These could be posted on the fridge or printed on file cards, and placed in a box for reference.

Do's and Don'ts to Remember

• Keep instruction time short, perhaps five to ten minutes.
• Choose only one spelling concept to focus on, for

example, a topical word, a suffix, a rhyming pattern, or a dictionary skill. Do not feel obliged to have a list of words to study.

You may deal with only one word, you may have a short list of sight words (for example, months, scientific terminology), you may build a category with dozens of words. It is the concept you are teaching. You may work on an ending, for example, do more words end in *eat* (ch*eat*, *neat*, etc.) or *ate* (*gate*, *inflate*, *implicate*, etc.).

• Focus on investigation and problem solving, not memorization.
• Always link words in a spelling context. Use words that share a spelling pattern, a meaning link, or derivation.
• Choose words and concepts your child is likely to need in his or her writing.
• Encourage your child to apply new learning as quickly as possible. This might be in proof-reading for a specific spelling pattern, collecting or categorizing words, solving puzzles, using reference materials, reading, or researching.
• Do not make a test the goal of spelling learning.
• Encourage your child to relate the spelling concept to his or her own writing.

How to Help Spelling Learning

• Focus on spelling only at appropriate times. Short mini-lessons are appropriate.
• Teach your child that spelling is a thinking activity, and

not a memory activity.

• Show your child when, where, and why spelling matters – and when it is less important.

• Encourage any attempt your child makes to spell.

• Provide information about words when the opportunity arises.

• Provide opportunities for your child to share finished stories with aunts, uncles, grandparents, and friends of the family.

• Point out interesting facts about links between words, word origins, and so on.

• Help your child link words into "word families" which have the same spelling pattern.

• Talk about one spelling concept or pattern at a time.

• Draw attention to groups of words that share a spelling pattern.

• Encourage games and puzzles that involve words.

• Encourage your child to talk about strategies that help.

• Help with proof-reading for specific things, such as plurals.

• Share information about the function of spelling patterns. As an example, an *er* ending often indicates a person who does something (*baker, teacher*).

• Nurture a growing awareness of word meanings, origins, and derivations.

• Demonstrate and encourage the use of reference materials.

• Form your expectations according to what your child knows and is capable of learning, not according to standardized norms.

• Build a record of what your child knows about spelling, rather than what she or he doesn't know. Share this with him or her.

> Little and often is a good rule for spelling instruction.

How to Hinder Spelling Learning

• Expect to see accurate spelling at early stages in learning.
• Impress on your child that spelling is of primary importance in writing.
• Teach your child that all words have to be memorized.
• Expect your child to look up all their errors in the dictionary.
• Require corrected spelling in every piece of writing.
• Teach spelling by using lists of words which do not share a spelling pattern or generalization. This leaves memorization as the only strategy.
• Measure spelling proficiency by scores on tests.
• Draw conclusions about spelling ability by evaluating first-draft writing.
• Downgrade your child's writing because of spelling errors.
• Focus on your child's weaknesses.
• Set lists of words to be memorized.

5. Evaluation

Recognizing Growth

One of the best ways to improve your child's confidence as a speller is to point out areas of growth. We have provided a number of examples of children's work with information on "what the child knows," and then, "what can be taught." As you work with your child, we hope you can identify growth with reference to these samples.

Example 1

Morna

What the child knows:

– a picture can preserve and convey meaning.
– how to print her name in upper-case letters.
– writing is a way of preserving and communicating meaning.
– meaning is represented by squiggles on the page.
– in order to write, you put these squiggles in rows.

What can reasonably be taught:

– ask the child to "read" the story.
– reinforce the fact that the use of correct letters in the name enables others to read it. Mention the fact that authors always put their names on their work.
– ask about the story told in the picture, so she will generate language to explain, describe, and so on.
– below the picture, print a sentence the author has dictated. Read the "story" back. This will show her that language can be preserved by print.
– determine if she knows any other letters, and help her to write them.
– suggest that she visit the library to find some alphabet books.
– do not pressure her to have the story written; sometimes appreciate art for art's sake.
– provide many more opportunities for her to compose meaning through picture.

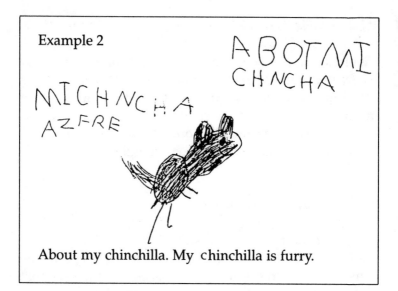

Example 2

ABOTMI
CHNCHA

MICHNCHA
AZFRE

About my chinchilla. My chinchilla is furry.

What the child knows:

– every syllable of a word must be represented by letters.
– some sounds are represented by two letters, *ch*.
– consonant sounds *b, t, m, n, z, f, r*.
– vowel sounds *o, a, i, e*.
– this piece has a title, a story, and an illustration. They are separate parts of the writing.

What can reasonably be taught:

– read back the title and story, pointing to each syllable as you go. Reinforce her concept that every syllable is represented.
– begin using the word, *word*. Ask her to tell you where

the word *my* ends, and the word, *chinchilla* begins. Show that in books, words are written with spaces in between to make them easier to read. Ask her how many words she has written in her story. Suggest that next time she might try to put spaces between her words. If, on the next occasion, she puts large dots between words, praise this. It will be a short phase.

Example 3

I whis I cieD Be SUPERMan
But i Cant avry time I
qsc goD to ttn me in to SUPERMan
It Duzint Wirk.

Grade One
Seven Years old.

I whis I cied be Superman

What the child knows:

– how to write a complete narrative.
– to represent all the sounds of every word.
– 16 out of 23 words are spelled correctly (70%).
– high-frequency words: *i, be, but, me, in, to, it.*
– attempted contraction: *cant.*

– long vowel, silent *e*: *time*.
– compound word: *Superman*.

What can reasonably be taught:

– *asc*: *c* and *k* make the same sound. At the end of words it is almost always *k*. Several other words share this pattern: *mask, task, flask* ...
– *whis*: *sh* sound. Many other words share this pattern.
– vowel sound patterns.

Until he has learned more about vowels, learning the sight word *could*, along with *would* and *should* is probably too much for this child. Contractions and punctuation should also be left until later.

Example 4

I was desprat to join the most coolest club in scool, I just had to they said I could but I had to stay overnight at the old deserted mantion that everybody said was haunted. I will I told them. As I enterd the mantion I heard a shreek from upstairs. It was probably just an owl I said to myself, or was it. The mantion was old and dusty. The floors creeked and the wind howled. I went up the stairs very slowly afraid that the stairs would cave in. When I got to the top of the stairs. I saw somthing in the room in front of me. I ran in to the room out of coureosoty, there was nothing there and it was cold in that room how strange. Oh well I better get some

---

> rest. Later I heard a scream it woke me up. I finally built up enough courage to look out the window. Althou I could see clearly in the moonlight none was there. Sudenly the fog moved in, and the trees swad even though there was no wind.

What the child knows:

– how to create mood and build suspense in a narrative. This is the first page of a lengthy story.
– use of full stops.
– of 187 words in the story, 174 are spelled correctly (93%).
– a large number of irregular words: *they, said, could, night, haunted, afraid, heard, some, built, enough, courage, though, there.*
– compound words: *everybody, overnight, moonlight.*
– endings to root words: *coolest, deserted, haunted, howled, slowly, moved.*
– *mantion*: the most common *shun* ending.

What can reasonably be taught:

– the use of commas as an aid to the reader.
– sight word *school*. Other words share the *sch* spelling pattern, but they are not words she is likely to need.
– *entrd*, the pattern for adding *d* or *ed* for past tenses. She might be able to self-correct here, as she is usually good with added endings.
– *though* is spelled correctly, but *althou* is not. She could be helped to see a link between these two words.

– *shreek/creeked*, she has chosen the most common way of spelling the *ee* sound. She might collect words which belong to the same patterns as *shriek* and *creak*.

– words like *desperate*, *mansion*, and *curiosity* could be given if the writing is to be edited in a further draft. Each belongs to a word pattern, but they are not words that are likely to be useful at this stage.

Example 5

The Boy Hwo Found a 20 Doller Bill
   One day I was rideing my bike down the sreet and I saw a loterey ticket. It said if you win you get 1 million dollers. I rode my bike home and gave the lotery ticket to my mom and ran to tell my frends. Wile I was gone to my frends house, the lottery men lochated my house and came over to my house. We won the lottery and now I am in the richest house of them all.

What the child knows:

– how to write a very simple narrative. It has logic and sequence, but no anecdote, description, and so on.
– of 87 words, 76 are spelled correctly discounting repeated errors (87%).
– several irregular words: *one, saw, was, said, won.*
– vowel combination *ou*: f*ou*nd, h*ou*se.
– other vowel combinations: *boy, now, saw, you.*
What could reasonably be taught:

– *wh* – give him the group of question words – *who, what, where, when, why.* Add *while.* He could keep these as a cheat sheet until he has memorized them.

– *rideing,* drop the *e* before adding endings. This generalization can apply to many words.

– ask him to look at the word *sreet* to see if he can self-correct.

– sight words – *dollar, lottery, million, friends, located* – may be given for editing purposes if a final draft is to be written. This child needs to know how to elaborate and expand his story, as well as learning about spelling patterns.

Example 6

Hello.

Well, I am *writting* to you in order to *determain* the *quallity* of my spelling.

I do have my days *were* I can spell anything, and then there are days that I can't spell a thing. Right now it's a *meadoaker* day.

I am a truck driver so my *writting* and spelling are not practised as much as I'd like. In fact there are times that I lack the confidence to go forth and *conquere* the BA of life. It's funny, I graduated from school, <u>done</u> a year and a half of a management systems program at Lakehead University, and I still cannot spell or express (<u>myself</u>) in proper English. <u>or so</u> called the norm.

My *personel* outlook these days is possibly to go back to school. However I'd like very much to beat

---

this English thing first. I am also at a stage in life where I am not sure of what I'd like to do with the rest of my life. So currently I am exploring avenues, such as teaching, or maybe finishing my BA in *Bussiness* and attempting to get on with a company as a person who isn't a figure head but is a big part of making the company run. I like to be the center of the *cayous*.

I wonder if your job of defining my spelling problem is greatly <u>influence</u> by my poor hand *writting*.

Well, I have definitely talked <u>alot</u> about myself. I'd like to thank you for the time you are putting forth to help me with my problem. So thanks.

Dan

Letter analysis: nine spelling errors (in italics); five grammar errors (underlined)

This letter was written by an articulate and educated young adult who feels he has a serious problem in spelling. In fact, 96 per cent of the words he has written are spelled correctly, but for the reader the errors in spelling and grammar seem to dominate the text. How may Dan be helped?

First, Dan needs to feel more confident as a speller by recognizing how much he does know:

– he spelled correctly many words which often cause problems: *practised, confidence, graduated, management, possibly, currently, avenues, wonder.*

– he is able to use alphabetic principles to create readable spellings for words he does not know.

– he does not avoid words like *mediocre* and *chaos* because he does not know how to spell them.

– he had written *determain* because he thought it sounded like *remain*. This was a conscious effort to use a known spelling in order to come up with a possible spelling for an unfamiliar word.

Dan was not aware that he had a problem with doubling. Knowing that doubling a consonant makes the previous vowel short may correct his spelling of *writting*, and help with many other words.

Dan needs to learn to make meaning connections:

– he did not know that he confused *were* and *where*. Awareness of these words may help him to proof-read for this error.

– he was able to spell *busy* with no problem, but had never connected it with *business*. It had never occurred to him to connect words in this way.

– he had no memory of *mediocre*, so made a prediction which could be read. Dan was advised to link *medi* with *mini* and *maxi*. He immediately recognized the meaning link among these three words. *Ocre* is uncommon, and needs to be memorized.

– *cayous* was another invention. He was fascinated to see *chaos* written down, and interested in the Greek origin. He was also shown *chasm*, *choir*, *chorus*, *chameleon*, and *character* as a rare spelling group.

– he had written *conquere* to rhyme with *were*. He learned that *er* is a verb function ending, as in *canter*, *wonder*, and a more common ending than *ere*, such as in *sister*, *water*, *teacher*.

– he had written *personel* based on *personnel*, which he has probably seen more often than *personal*. Correct pronunciation of these two might help him to remember the difference. He made up his own mnemonic device – a person called Al.

Dan was also advised to ask a friend to help with proof-reading important pieces, such as a letter of application to a university.

Dan was excited by talking about his writing and the analysis of his spelling patterns, and was empowered by his new learning. He could now proof-read and look for some specific errors, and had learned new ways to work out and remember spellings. Above all, he had learned that there are strategies for making decisions about spellings.

Dan is a keen writer. He kept a journal on his 46-day trip to Alaska. When writing for himself as an audience he was more relaxed and made fewer spelling errors. Talking about his successes and his errors seemed to open new doors for Dan. He gave us permission to reprint his letter because of a desire to help others who may have a similar problem. He has made a commitment to being accurate in his written English. We wish him well.

When we look at samples of writing our first reaction is often to ask the age or school year of the writer. This is because we have certain expectations, or norms, against which we judge the worth of the composition, handwriting, spelling, complexity of language, level of vocabulary, and so on. Knowing how a child ranks among others of the same age may well be valid for certain purposes, but for assessing the progress of an individual or deciding what kind of help a child needs, it is less than useful.

To be useful, information about spelling must be specific and detailed. *Knowing the kind of errors a child makes is more useful than knowing how many mistakes.* Just as the child will learn about spellings by recognizing patterns and making generalizations, so we can help by assessing which patterns and generalizations the child is familiar with, and which need to be taught. Spelling errors, other than typographical ones done in the course of a hasty draft, are not usually made at random – some logic is used to arrive at a particular combination of letters. Finding out *why* children make misspellings can give us a window on their understanding of the logic of spelling.

Talking to Your Child's Teacher

What is it that you, as parents, want to read about your child on reports? There are three main questions for which you need answers.

1. Does my child have a good attitude towards work and learning?
2. Is my child performing at a reasonable level of achievement for his or her age group?
3. Has my child made progress since the last reporting period?

These three points might provide a framework for any interview you have with your child's teacher. With these in mind, here are some ways you can structure an interview to give you the answers you need.

• Share your observations. What is your impression of your child's attitude towards writing and spelling? Does your child bring writing home to share with you? How does your family respond to the writing? Does your child write at home? What kinds of writing do other family members do at home?

• Ask detailed questions. Look at the writing your child does in school. Ask the teacher to show you evidence of growth and learning, both in your child's writing, and in classroom records.

• Ask for suggestions about how you can best support the classroom teaching at home. If your child has difficulties, find out how you can help.

• Make notes about your discussion. You will need to remind yourself later of any suggestions the teacher has made. You can also follow up on your discussion at a future date.

• Share your discoveries with your child. Be positive and encouraging.

Don't feel you have to wait for parents' evening to talk to your child's teacher. Most teachers will welcome your interest. They want you to understand what they are doing in the classroom, and are eager to get you involved. Learning is a partnership: child, parent, teacher – in that order of importance.

6. Conclusion

The experiences most of us had in our schooling led us to believe that spelling is a matter of memorizing words. We now know that this is not the case. Memorization plays a part, but there are other skills necessary for a person to be a successful speller.

We have outlined our beliefs about spelling skills, and the best way for children to learn and practise them. Here is a brief summary to bring it together for you.

• Children will learn to spell in the same way they learned to talk – by approximating what they see around them, and gradually getting closer to standard English.

• Children learn to spell in order to write. The more writing they do, the more they can learn about spelling. Anything that makes them reluctant to write will work against spelling learning.

• Spelling is a skill of constructing words, not of memorizing words. Therefore children who learn to "invent" spellings know more about our spelling system and are ultimately better spellers than those who have only tried to memorize words.

• Children learn about spelling even when they make errors. They do not write letters at random; they reason logically, and use the best information they have to build words. It is by analyzing children's errors that we know what they need to learn.

• Invented spelling doesn't "stick." If children read a lot they will see standard spellings far more often than their invented spellings. From these models, and from the help we give, children will build their knowledge of how words are constructed, gradually come closer to standard spelling, and abandon their primitive inventions.

• Good spellers have three main strategies for spelling:

1. Matching sounds with letters. Many words can be spelled this way. Parts of all words can be spelled this way.
2. Considering how a word is used. For example, a past tense is spelled *ed* even if it sounds like *id* or *t* (waited, jumped).
3. Considering the meaning of a word. For example, you can remember the spelling of *here* if you connect it with other location words – *there, where. Please* and *pleasant* have the same vowel combination, even though they are pronounced differently. It is the meaning that gives you the correct spelling, not the sound.

Young children will learn 1. first. Later, they will become increasingly proficient in using the other two strategies.

• It will take children a long time to learn enough to become reasonably proficient spellers. For a number of years, they will be writing words they cannot spell. Therefore, when we evaluate their spelling learning we are not necessarily looking to see how many words they get right or wrong, but whether they are learning new concepts and spelling patterns.

• Spelling is important. However, it is only a part of the total writing process. With writing and spelling we teach one skill at a time to ensure better learning. Therefore in some pieces of writing, spelling will not be a primary focus; it may not be mentioned. At other times, spelling will be a focus, and we can direct children's attention to specific words and concepts.

• Children who are anxious about making spelling errors are reluctant to write. As a result, they learn neither composition nor spelling.

Even a beginner writer should be able to explain to you why some writing has spelling corrected and some does not. Your child should also be able to talk about methods to figure out spellings, ways to use the dictionary, and so on. If your child does not understand the what, the why, and the how of spelling she or he cannot learn it successfully.

If we have a true understanding of the writing process, we can put spelling in perspective. Once we raise children's awareness of the way words are constructed, and of the interrelationship of language and spelling, we can expect that their knowledge of patterns and anomalies will continue to grow and fascinate. That learning will be a lifelong affair is surely the ultimate goal.

Notes
About Your Child's Difficulties and Progress

Notes

Notes

Notes

Notes

Notes

Notes

OTHER BOOKS PUBLISHED BY PICCADILLY PRESS

A-Z GUIDE TO YOUR CHILD'S BEHAVIOUR
Compiled by the faculty of the Children's National
    Medical Center

This guide will help parents understand the origins,
motivations, meanings and functions of their child's
development.

*"Written in such a reasonable tone and offers so much sound
advice ... "*
    Books for Children

GETTING PREGNANT AND STAYING PREGNANT
Diana Raab

*"An excellent information source on the complex issues and
decisions of infertility and high-risk pregnancy ..."*
    Booklist

WHAT WORRIES WOMEN MOST?
Dr Sarah Brewer

*"For all addicts of 'Dear Doctor' columns in the women's press,
this is a must. Written in simple, snappy style ... "*
    Good Book Guide

Just published:

PROBLEM PERIODS: Causes, Symptoms and Relief
Dr Caroline Shreeve

Few women can escape problems with their period. This book examines the whole spectrum of menstrual problems that can arise between the first period and menopause.

ARE YOU EXPECTING TOO MUCH FROM YOUR
CHILD?
Dr Fiona Subotsky

Every child deserves to be accepted for who they are, not who their parents want them to be. This book draws parents' attention to their own behaviour and expectations, which might have a negative effect on their child's behaviour.

Coming soon:

CHILDCARE: A Guide for the Working Parent
Geraldine Bown

Childcare is the cause of endless concern for working parents, whatever the age of their child or children. And it's one area where a parent can't afford to make a mistake; this comprehensive book should ensure that you don't.

NATURAL REMEDIES: Common Ailments Cured
Gordon Sambidge

This elegant book is now available in paperback.

"This is the book to reach for when you need to cure an ailment or for first aid. Full of practical wisdom, the remedies it suggests can be easily obtained or found around the home ... no household should be without this holistic guide to health and well-being."
Janet Balaskas – The Active Birth Centre

NATURAL REMEDIES FOR YOUR CAT
Christopher Day

Qualified veterinary surgeon and leading homoeopathic vet, Christopher Day, gives advice on the treatment of many ailments, explains the remedies, and discusses diet and life style.

" ... a beautifully illustrated handbook ... "
Daily Express